A PRACTICAL GUIDE TO THE MASTERY
OF PORTUGUESE

PORTUGUESE
Verbs & Essentials of Grammar

Sue Tyson-Ward

PASSPORT BOOKS
NTC/Contemporary Publishing Group

Preface

This new addition to the *Essentials* series presents the major grammatical concepts of the Portuguese language in accordance with current practices in both Portugal and Brazil. The *1971 Acordo Ortográfico,* an agreement standardizing much of the spelling throughout the Portuguese-speaking world, was to have been updated recently. As this book goes to print, the final revision still has not been approved by all parties. This work points out the differences in grammar between the Portuguese of mainland Portugal and Brazil and, as such, is a useful guide to anyone having contact with either country.

As evidenced by the first section of the book, great emphasis is placed on mastery of verbs, their conjugations, and uses. Grammar and sentence structure are presented in easily understood contexts. New material is used in such a way that it is based upon and builds on material previously presented, so that the student can progress with ease through the various sections. Each individual grammar point is dealt with in a step-by-step way, enabling the student to fully grasp a concept before moving on.

A major advantage of *Portuguese Verbs and Essentials of Grammar* is that, contrary to many foreign-language textbooks, complete grammar explanations are contained in each section. Topics are not scattered throughout the text; therefore, both teacher and student can easily locate the information they need.

Following each grammatical explanation are numerous examples. These clearly illustrate the point in question, and can be used as a basis for further work by the student. The lists of verbs and vocabularies of theme-based words and phrases provide material for use in creative exercises, oral work, and compositions.

As a reference text, *Portuguese Verbs and Essentials of Grammar* can be used by individual students for study or review, or by the teacher and the class as a supplement to other language textbooks. Because of the logical order in which concepts are presented, this book can be used on any level, from junior high school through college, as well as in adult education courses.

Library of Congress Cataloging-in-Publication Data
is available from the United States Library of Congress

Cover design by Nick Panos

Published by Passport Books
A division of NTC/Contemporary Publishing Group, Inc.
4255 West Touhy Avenue, Lincolnwood (Chicago), Illinois 60712-1975 U.S.A.
Printed in the United States of America
International Standard Book Number: 0-8442-4698-0
6 7 8 9 VRS/VRS 0 4 3 2

Contents

Part Two: Essentials of Grammar

Part One:
Portuguese Verbs

1. Pronunciation

The Alphabet

The Portuguese alphabet contains twenty-three simple letters, plus three signs, or double letters, representing simple sounds. The letters *k* (*capa* in Portugal, *cá* in Brazil), *w* (*vê duplo* in Portugal, *dábliu* in Brazil), and *y* (*ípsilon*) are not found in native Portuguese words, although they occur in abbreviated forms of metric measure, chemical symbols, and foreign loan words.

The letters are all masculine in gender.

a	*á*	i	*i*	q	*quê*
b	*bê*	j	*jota*	r	*erre*
c	*cê*	l	*ele*	s	*esse*
ch	*cê agá*	lh	*ele agá*	t	*tê*
d	*dê*	m	*eme*	u	*u*
e	*é*	n	*ene*	v	*vê*
f	*efe*	o	*ó*	x	*xis*
g	*gê*	p	*pê*	z	*zê*
h	*agá*				

A maiúsculo	capital A	` (à) *o acento grave*	grave accent
a minúsculo	small a	~ (ã) *o til*	tilde
ç cê cedilha	c cedilla	¨ (ü) *a diérese, o trema*	dieresis
´ (á) *o acento agudo*	acute accent		
^ (ê) *o acento circunflexo*	circumflex accent		

The following is a broad outline of Portuguese pronunciation. The approximate pronunciation of each letter is like that found in the English word that follows it.

Vowels

a (stressed)	father: *mal, falar*
	The most common *a* sound in Brazil
a (unstressed)	abide: *saber, bica*
ã	sang: *maçã, irmã, canto*
	This is a nasal vowel.
e (stressed)	sell: *zero, perto*

e (unstressed)	sadden: *pedir, pesar, carne*
	In Brazil, when at end of word, like vowel sound in "bee"
é	sell: *José, café*
ê	they: *francês, vê*
i (stressed)	lean: *vida, partida*
i (unstressed)	cigar: *dizer, migrar*
o (stressed)	law: *envelope, nova*
o (unstressed)	root: *livro, sapato*
ô	oh: *estômago*
	The most common *o* sound in Brazil
u (stressed)	root: *tubo, durmo*
u (unstressed)	mull: *mulher*
	The sound is almost nasal.

Consonants

b	boy: *bonito, sobre*
c	Before *e, i,* or when written with a cedilla, like "sit": *cem, estação*
c	Before *a, o, or u,* like "cat": *comer, cada*
ch	show: *achar, chão*
d	dad: *dar, mundo*
	In Portugal, if *d* appears in the middle of a word and does not follow *l, m,* or *n,* it is pronounced much more softly: *fado, seda.*
	In Brazil, *de* and *di* are often pronounced like "gee": *cidade, difícil.*
f	fan: *falar, defender*
g	Before *e, i,* like *s* in "measure": *geléia, agir*
g	Before *a, o, u,* like "get": *pagar, bigode*
h	Always silent: *há, hotel*
j	Like the *s* in "measure": *junho, vejo*
l	land: *livro, sol*
	In Brazil, *l* following a vowel tends to become a *w* sound: *total.*
lh	Like *lli* in "million": *olhar, trabalhar*
m	man: *animal, meu*
	When at the end of a syllable and preceded by a vowel, the vowel is nasalized.
	At the end of a word, *m* is barely pronounced: *tem.*
n	not: *nada, caneta*
	When at the end of a syllable, preceded by a vowel and followed by a consonant, the vowel is nasalized: *senso, alento.*
nh	Like the *ni* in "onion": *vinho, junho*
	The *n* is barely pronounced.

p	pan: *para, aparecer*
q	quarter: *quando, quarto*
	Always followed by *u*
	When followed by *e* or *i*, the *u* is silent unless it carries a dieresis: *quem, máquina.*
r	In Portugal, initial *r* and *rr* in the middle of a word are rolled, as in Spanish.
	In Brazil, they are guttural, from the back of the throat, like a very hard *h*: *Rio, cigarro.*
	Single *r* following another letter is flipped, as in Spanish: *branco, perguntar.*
	In much of Brazil, final *r* is dropped.
s	Initial *s*, *s* after a consonant, or double *ss*, like "sit": *sol, posso*
	When between two vowels, as in "zoo": *caso, mesa*
	When at end of a word or before *c, f, p, q,* or *t*, like "show": *livros, gostar*
	In parts of Brazil, *s* in these positions is the same as the initial *s* sound.
t	tell: *tudo, setenta*
	In Brazil, *te* and *ti* are often pronounced like "cheer": *noite, tipo.*
v	van: *vida, envelope*
x	At the beginning of a word, before a consonant, and sometimes between two vowels, as in "show": *xarope, baixa, explicar*
	Also between two vowels, as in "son": *proximidade, auxiliar*
	When *ex* precedes a vowel, as in "zoo": *exame, exibir*
	In some foreign or more scholarly words, as in "taxi": *táxi, fluxo, anexo*
z	At the beginning of a word, or between vowels, like "zoo": *fazer, zero*
	At the end of a word, like "show": *faz, luz*
	Final *z* in Brazil is often like the *s* sound in "measure."

Accent or Stress

Usually verb forms ending in *am* and *em* and other words ending in *a, e, o, em,* and *ens,* stress the penultimate, or next-to-the-last, syllable *(casa, comem).* Words ending in *i, u,* diphthongs, consonants, and nasal vowels stress the last syllable *(estação, hotel).*

If the syllable stressed in a word deviates from these norms, a written accent is required. Written accents can be acute (´), indicating an open vowel sound *(café, pássaro),* and circumflex (ˆ), expressing a closed sound *(você, pêssego).* Both of these are used to indicate stress.

There is also a grave accent (`` ` ``), which indicates a contraction of the preposition *a*, either with the feminine definite articles *(a + a = à, a + as = às)* or with demonstrative adjectives or pronouns (see Chapter 21) beginning with *a (a + aquele = àquele, à + aquelas = àquelas,* etc.). The tilde (~), usually on a stressed syllable, nasalizes the vowel.

Diphthongs

A, e, and *o* are strong vowels and form separate syllables within a word: *po-e-ma.*

U and *i* are weak vowels and, when combined with a strong vowel or another weak vowel, form what is known as a diphthong. (Note that a weak vowel can only be separated from a strong one by means of a written accent: *saída.* The resulting vowel combination is called a hiatus.)

Oral Diphthongs

ai	eye: *mais*	
au	now: *pausa*	
ei	gate: *maneira*	
eu	*ay-oo: comeu*	
iu	*ee-oo: partiu*	
oi	boy: *boi*	
ou	know: *cenoura*	
ui	sweet: *Rui.* The *u* sounds almost like a *w* in this diphthong.	

Nasal Diphthongs

There are no exact equivalents to these sounds in English. They are focused forward toward the roof of the mouth, and resonate in the nose.

ãe	fly: *mãe*
ãi	fly: *cãibra*
ão	clown: *mão*
õe	toy: *informações*

Punctuation Marks

,	a vírgula		( )	os parênteses
.	o ponto (final)		'	o apóstrofo
:	dois pontos		-	o hífen
;	o ponto e vírgula		" "	as aspas
?	o ponto de interrogação		!	o ponto de exclamação

2. Regular Verbs— Indicative Tenses

Subject Pronouns

The subject of a verb is the person (or thing) carrying out an action, and can be represented by a pronoun in the first, second, or third person, singular or plural, as follows:

	Singular			Plural	
1.	**eu**	I	**nós**	we	
2.	**tu**	you	**vós**	you	
3.	**ele**	he/it	**eles** *(m.)*	they	
	ela	she/it	**elas** *(f.)*	they	
	você	you	**vocês**	you	

Tu, the familiar form of "you," is used with close friends, family, children, and pets. In many areas of Brazil, *você* is used with everyone. Through the influence of Brazilian soap operas *(telenovelas),* the *você* form is starting to be heard in Portugal among young people. The *vós* form is considered outdated, and is generally heard only in church services, public speeches, and the conversation of older speakers living in remote regions. *Vocês* is the accepted plural "you."

Note: Portuguese subject pronouns do not have to be used with the verb, since in most cases, the verb ending denotes the subject. However, to avoid any ambiguity, pronouns should be used with the third-person forms, unless there is no doubt as to who or what the subject is.

Conjugations

All Portuguese verbs fall into three groups, known as conjugations. "Conjugation" is also the term used for those verb endings that indicate who is performing the action, at what time, and under what circumstances.

The three conjugations are:

1. Verbs ending in **-ar** (the most common group)   **falar** to speak
2. Verbs ending in **-er**   **comer** to eat
3. Verbs ending in **-ir**   **partir** to leave

There are also a number of irregular verbs (see Chapters 8, 11, and 12).

The verb forms with the above endings are known as infinitives. The infinitive is the form of the verb that appears first in dictionaries. When the infinitive ending *(-ar, -er,* or *-ir)* is removed, what is left is known as the *stem*. To conjugate the verb, the appropriate ending is added to this stem.

The Indicative Mood

The indicative mood *(indicativo)* is the verb formation used most often. It commonly denotes straightforward situations, such as events that have actually occurred, and is found in a variety of tenses. The subjunctive mood, as will be discussed later, is used in other circumstances.

Tenses of the Indicative

1. Present   *Presente*
2. Imperfect   *Pretérito imperfeito*
3. Preterite   *Pretérito perfeito*
4. Simple Pluperfect   *Pretérito mais-que-perfeito*
5. Future   *Futuro imperfeito*
6. Conditional   *Condicional imperfeito*

The Present

The present tense in Portuguese is used for actions or states happening as the speaker is talking, for emphatic speech, for description of habitual actions or states, and for expressing the future. Therefore, **eu falo** can mean:

"I speak," "I am speaking," "I do speak," "I will speak."

First Conjugation, *-ar*

To form the present tense of first-conjugation verbs, add the following endings to the stem of the verb.

falar, to speak
I speak, do speak, am speaking, will speak; you speak, etc.

	Singular			Plural	
eu	**fal**o	I speak	**nós**	**fal**amos	we speak
tu	**fal**as	you speak	**vós**	**fal**ais	you speak
ele	**fal**a	he speaks	**eles**	**fal**am	they speak
ela	**fal**a	she speaks	**elas**	**fal**am	they speak
você	**fal**a	you speak	**vocês**	**fal**am	you speak

A noun, pronoun, or combination of both, may be used as the subject of the verb. Remember: subject pronouns are really only needed to avoid ambiguity or for emphasis.

Falo português.	I speak Portuguese.
Maria, *tu* **falas bem inglês.**	You speak English well, Mary.
Você **fala italiano.**	You speak Italian.
Márcia e *eu* **falamos juntas.**	Marcia and I are speaking together.

Negative Form

To form the negative of a verb, place *não* directly before it.

Não **falo inglês.**	I do not speak English.
Pedro *não* **fala bem.**	Peter does not speak well.

Interrogative Form

To form a simple question, just raise the intonation of your voice at the end of the sentence. Inversion of subject and verb also takes place, but not so frequently. The words "do" and "does" are not expressed in Portuguese.

Fala inglês?	Do you speak English?
Falam eles?	Are they speaking?

(For more on negatives and interrogatives, see Chapter 25.)

Sample Verbs of the First Conjugation

acabar	to finish	jogar	to play
andar	to walk	lavar	to wash
brincar	to play	limpar	to clean
buscar	to seek	mandar	to send
cantar	to sing	morar	to live
começar	to begin	nadar	to swim
ensinar	to teach	notar	to notice
estudar	to study	pagar	to pay
falar	to speak	parar	to stop
fechar	to close	regressar	to return (to a place)
ganhar	to win	reservar	to reserve
gostar	to like	saltar	to jump
jantar	to dine	trabalhar	to work

Second Conjugation, *-er*

comer, to eat
I eat, do eat, am eating, will eat; you eat, etc.

Singular		Plural	
eu	com*o*	nós	com*emos*
tu	com*es*	vós	com*eis*
ele	com*e*	eles	com*em*
ela	com*e*	elas	com*em*
você	com*e*	vocês	com*em*

Como **frutas.**	I eat fruit.
João não *come* **peixe.**	John does not eat fish.
Você *come* **carne?**	Do you eat meat?
Comemos **muito pão.**	We eat a lot of bread.
Os meninos não *comem* **bem.**	The boys do not eat well.

Sample Verbs of the Second Conjugation

aprender	to learn	escrever	to write
atender	to answer (the telephone)	fender	to split, to crack
bater	to beat	ferver	to boil
beber	to drink	meter	to put in
comer	to eat	ofender	to offend
compreender	to understand	preencher	to fill out (forms)
correr	to run	responder	to answer, to reply
debater	to debate	surpreender	to surprise
dever	to owe; ought, must	vender	to sell
escolher	to choose	viver	to live

Third Conjugation, *-ir*

partir, to leave
I leave, do leave, am leaving, will leave; you leave, etc.

	Singular		Plural
eu	**part***o*	nós	**part***imos*
tu	**part***es*	vós	**part***is*
ele	**part***e*	eles	**part***em*
ela	**part***e*	elas	**part***em*
você	**part***e*	vocês	**part***em*

Parto **amanhã.**	I'm leaving tomorrow.
A Ana *parte* **às seis horas.**	Anne leaves at six o'clock.
Eduardo e eu não *partimos* **hoje.**	Edward and I are not leaving today.
Elas *partem* **de Nova York.**	They leave from New York.

Sample Verbs of the Third Conjugation

abrir	to open	**invadir**	to invade
admitir	to admit; to accept	**omitir**	to omit
aplaudir	to applaud	**subir**	to go up
assistir (a)	to attend	**transmitir**	to transmit
decidir	to decide	**unir**	to unite

The Imperfect

This is the first of the simple past tenses in Portuguese. It is used to express an action that was happening in the past, in a continuous manner, as well as for repeated or habitual past actions. It is also used for descriptive effect, especially for background to a story or event that is being narrated. It is not as well defined in terms of time as the preterite.

The imperfect is formed by adding the following endings to the stem of the verb.

falar
I was speaking, used to speak; you were speaking, etc.

fal*ava*	**fal***ávamos*
fal*avas*	**fal***áveis*
fal*ava*	**fal***avam*

comer
I was eating, used to eat; you were eating, etc.

com*ia*	com*íamos*
com*ias*	com*íeis*
com*ia*	com*iam*

partir
I was leaving, used to leave; you were leaving, etc.

part*ia*	part*íamos*
part*ias*	part*íeis*
part*ia*	part*iam*

Observe that *-er* and *-ir* verbs have identical endings in the imperfect.

A Maria *nadava* **todos os dias.**	Mary used to swim every day.
Eu *falava* **com a professora.**	I was talking to the teacher.
Os senhores Paiva *viviam* **em Paris.**	Mr. and Mrs. Paiva used to live in Paris.
Chovia **muito e o vento** *estava* **forte.**	It was raining a lot, and the wind was strong.
Morávamos **numa casa grande.**	We used to live in a big house.

The Preterite

This tense serves the purpose of expressing past actions that have been completed, and can often be used in contrast with the imperfect tense. It is a more strictly defined past tense than the imperfect.

The preterite is formed by adding these endings to the stem.

falar
I spoke, did speak; you spoke, etc.

fal*ei*	fal*ámos,* fal*amos (Br.)*
fal*aste*	fal*astes*
fal*ou*	fal*aram*

comer
I ate, did eat; you ate, etc.

com*i*	com*emos*
com*este*	com*estes*
com*eu*	com*eram*

partir
I left, did leave; you left, etc.

part*i*	part*imos*
part*iste*	part*istes*
part*iu*	part*iram*

Note similar patterns in the three conjugations. This will be an aid to learning the preterite endings.

fal*aste*   **com***este*   **part***iste*

Ontem *falei* **com João.**	Yesterday I spoke to John.
Tu não *bebeste* **o vinho?**	Didn't you drink the wine?
A menina *vendeu* **o carro.**	The girl sold her car.
Abrimos **a loja.**	We opened the store.
Eles assistiam a televisão quando	They were watching television when
o telefone *tocou.*	the phone rang.

Simple Pluperfect

This tense describes action completed in the past prior to another past action. The simple pluperfect verb forms are used mostly in literary language, the compound pluperfect being utilized in everyday speech (see Chapter 3).

The simple pluperfect is formed by adding the following endings to the stem.

falar
I had spoken, you had spoken, etc.

fal*ara*	**fal***áramos*
fal*aras*	**fal***áreis*
fal*ara*	**fal***aram*

comer
I had eaten, you had eaten, etc.

com*era*	**com***éramos*
com*eras*	**com***éreis*
com*era*	**com***eram*

partir
I had left, you had left, etc.

part*ira*	part*íramos*
part*iras*	part*íreis*
part*ira*	part*iram*

Eu já *comera* **quando ela chegou.**   I had already eaten when she arrived.
O filme *terminara* **cedo.**   The film had ended early.
Partíramos **antes dela chegar.**   We had left before she arrived.

The Future

The future expresses action that has not yet happened. The future in English is formed by placing "will" or "shall" before a verb; in Portuguese it is formed by verb endings. The future is not used as much in Portuguese as in English, often being substituted by the present tense. The future is reserved for more emphatic situations. The endings for the future are straightforward, as there is only one set for all conjugations, which is added onto the whole infinitive of the verb.

falar
I will speak, etc.

falar*ei*	falar*emos*
falar*ás*	falar*eis*
falar*á*	falar*ão*

comer
I will eat, etc.

comer*ei*	comer*emos*
comer*ás*	comer*eis*
comer*á*	comer*ão*

partir
I will leave, etc.

partir*ei*	partir*emos*
partir*ás*	partir*eis*
partir*á*	partir*ão*

Falarei **com Pedro amanhã.**   I'll speak to Peter tomorrow.
Visitarás **o palácio?**   Will you visit the palace?
Eles *venderão* **a casa.**   They will sell their house.

The future can also express conjecture with respect to a present situation.

Onde *estará* **a senhora Oliveira?**   Where can Mrs. Oliveira be?
Pois, nesta hora, ela *estará* **em casa.**   Well, at this hour, she'll probably be at home.

The future can also be rendered by the use of the verb *ir* ("to go") + infinitive.

Vou fazer **muito trabalho amanhã.**   I'm going to do a lot of work tomorrow.

The Conditional

The conditional expresses a situation that is dependent on a previous past condition, sometimes explicit, other times understood implicitly.

There is only one set of endings, which are added to the infinitive of the verb.

falar		**comer**		**partir**	
I would speak, etc.		I would eat, etc.		I would leave, etc.	
falar*ia*	**falar***íamos*	**comer***ia*	**comer***íamos*	**partir***ia*	**partir***íamos*
falar*ias*	**falar***íeis*	**comer***ias*	**comer***íeis*	**partir***ias*	**partir***íeis*
falar*ia*	**falar***iam*	**comer***ia*	**comer***iam*	**partir***ia*	**partir***iam*

Gostaria **de visitar o museu.**   I would like to visit the museum.
Disse que *faria* **a tarefa amanhã.**   He said that he would do the job tomorrow.

The conditional is often substituted by the imperfect in Portuguese, especially in spoken language.

Gostava **de visitar o museu.**   I would like to visit the museum.

Checklist of Endings

Simple Tenses of the Indicative

		-ar		-er		-ir	
Present	*stem +*	**-o**	**-amos**	**-o**	**-emos**	**-o**	**-imos**
		-as	**-ais**	**-es**	**-eis**	**-es**	**-is**
		-a	**-am**	**-e**	**-em**	**-e**	**-em**
Imperfect	*stem +*	**-ava**	**-ávamos**	**-ia**	**-íamos**	**-ia**	**-íamos**
		-avas	**-áveis**	**-ias**	**-íeis**	**-ias**	**-íeis**
		-ava	**-avam**	**-ia**	**-iam**	**-ia**	**-iam**
Preterite	*stem +*	**-ei**	**-ámos, -amos** *(Br.)*	**-i**	**-emos**	**-i**	**-imos**
		-aste	**-astes**	**-este**	**-estes**	**-iste**	**-istes**
		-ou	**-aram**	**-eu**	**-eram**	**-iu**	**-iram**
Simple Pluperfect	*stem +*	**-ara**	**-áramos**	**-era**	**-éramos**	**-ira**	**-íramos**
		-aras	**-áreis**	**-eras**	**-éreis**	**-iras**	**-íreis**
		-ara	**-aram**	**-era**	**-eram**	**-ira**	**-iram**

		-ar, -er, -ir	
Future	*infinitive +*	**-ei**	**-emos**
		-ás	**-eis**
		-á	**-ão**
Conditional	*infinitive +*	**-ia**	**-íamos**
		-ias	**-íeis**
		-ia	**-iam**

Synopsis of the Simple Tenses

In a synopsis any one form of the verb is given in all the tenses.

falar—eu

Present	**falo**	I speak, am speaking
Imperfect	**falava**	I was speaking, used to speak
Preterite	**falei**	I spoke
Simple Pluperfect	**falara**	I had spoken
Future	**falarei**	I will speak
Conditional	**falaria**	I would speak

3. Perfect (Compound) Tenses

The perfect tenses in Portuguese are compound, that is, they are made up of more than one word. Perfect tenses are formed by placing the verb *ter* ("to have"), known as an auxiliary verb, before the past participle of any verb.

The perfect tenses are as follows:

1. Present Perfect   *Pretérito perfeito composto*
2. Pluperfect (Past Perfect)   *Pretérito mais-que-perfeito composto*
3. Future Perfect   *Futuro perfeito composto*
4. Conditional Perfect   *Condicional composto*

Formation of the Past Participle

To form the past participle of all regular verbs, add the following endings onto the stem of the verb:

-ar Verbs	-er Verbs	-ir Verbs
-ado	-ido	-ido
falar > falado, spoken	**comer > comido,** eaten	**partir > partido,** left

Irregular verbs usually have irregular past participles (see Chapter 8).

Present Perfect

The present perfect is formed by the present tense of the verb *ter* and the past participle of the main verb.

falar
I have spoken, have been speaking, etc.

tenho	fal*ado*	**temos**	fal*ado*
tens	fal*ado*	**tendes**	fal*ado*
tem	fal*ado*	**têm**	fal*ado*

Tenho falado **muito com ele ultimamente.**	I have been speaking with him a lot lately.
Não *tens comido* **muito estes dias.**	You have not eaten much recently.
Estes três anos *temos trabalhado* **muito.**	We have worked a lot these past three years.

Pluperfect (Past Perfect)

The pluperfect is formed by using the imperfect tense of the verb *ter* with the past participle of the main verb.

falar
I had spoken, you had spoken, etc.

tinha	**fal**ado	**tínhamos**	**fal**ado
tinhas	**fal**ado	**tínheis**	**fal**ado
tinha	**fal**ado	**tinham**	**fal**ado

A Maria *tinha estudado* **muito para o exame.**	Mary had studied a lot for the exam.
Não *tínhamos passado* **muito tempo no Rio.**	We had not spent much time in Rio.
Os professores *tinham aplaudido* **o esforço.**	The teachers had applauded the effort.

The auxiliary verb *haver* may take the place of *ter* in perfect tenses—most often in the pluperfect. It is commonly used only in archaic, literary, or poetic language.

Não *te havia cantado* **outrora.**	I had not sung to you in times past.

Future Perfect

This tense is formed by the future tense of the verb *ter* and the past participle of the main verb.

falar
I will have spoken, you will have spoken, etc.

terei	**fal**ado	**teremos**	**fal**ado
terás	**fal**ado	**tereis**	**fal**ado
terá	**fal**ado	**terão**	**fal**ado

Terei vendido **a casa antes de julho.**	I will have sold the house before July.
O João *terá chegado* **a tempo.**	John will have arrived on time.
Não *teremos terminado* **antes do prazo.**	We will not have finished before the deadline.

Conditional Perfect

This tense is formed by the conditional of the verb *ter* and the past participle of the main verb.

falar
I would have spoken, you would have spoken, etc.

teria	**fal***ado*	**teríamos**	**fal***ado*
terias	**fal***ado*	**teríeis**	**fal***ado*
teria	**fal***ado*	**teriam**	**fal***ado*

O Sr. Pereira *teria comprado* **a mesa, mas era muito cara.**	Mr. Pereira would have bought the table, but it was very expensive.
Que livro *terias escolhido***?**	Which book would you have chosen?
Não *teríamos visitado* **o castelo, mas o guia disse que valia a pena.**	We would not have visited the castle, but the guide said it was worth it.

Irregular Past Participles

All the irregular verbs in Chapter 8 are listed with their irregular past participles, but some verbs in Portuguese have two past participles. The regular one, formed as explained above, is used with *ter* and *haver* in the compound tenses, but the irregular forms function passively, almost as adjectives, with the verbs *ser* and *estar* ("to be"), as well as *ficar* ("to stay," "to remain"), *andar* ("to walk"), *ir* ("to go"), and *vir* ("to come"). Following are some verbs that act in this way. Where only one form is given, that form must be used exclusively.

		Regular	Irregular
abrir	to open	—	**aberto**
aceitar	to accept	**aceitado**	**aceito, aceite**
acender	to light	**acendido**	**aceso**
entregar	to hand over	**entregado**	**entregue**
enxugar	to dry	**enxugado**	**enxuto**
escrever	to write	—	**escrito**
expulsar	to expel	**expulsado**	**expulso**
ganhar	to win	—	**ganho**
gastar	to spend	—	**gasto**
limpar	to clean	**limpado**	**limpo**
matar	to kill	**matado**	**morto**
omitir	to omit	**omitido**	**omisso**
pagar	to pay	—	**pago**
prender	to arrest, to fasten	**prendido**	**preso**
romper	to tear	**rompido**	**roto**
soltar	to let loose	**soltado**	**solto**
suspender	to suspend	**suspendido**	**suspenso**

Checklist of Endings

Perfect Tenses of the Indicative

ter + past participle

Present Perfect	**tenho** _____	**temos** _____
	tens _____	**tendes** _____
	tem _____	**têm** _____

Pluperfect	**tinha** _____	**tínhamos** _____
(Past Perfect)	**tinhas** _____	**tínheis** _____
	tinha _____	**tinham** _____

Future Perfect	**terei** _____	**teremos** _____
	terás _____	**tereis** _____
	terá _____	**terão** _____

Conditional Perfect	**teria** _____	**teríamos** _____
	terias _____	**teríeis** _____
	teria _____	**teriam** _____

Synopsis of Perfect Tenses

falar—eu

Present Perfect	**tenho falado**	I have spoken, have been speaking
Pluperfect (Past Perfect)	**tinha falado**	I had spoken
Future Perfect	**terei falado**	I will have spoken
Conditional Perfect	**teria falado**	I would have spoken

4. Progressive Tenses

The progressive tenses express an action that is in progress, continuing, unfinished. In Portuguese, the progressive tenses are not used as much as in Spanish, and the range of tenses commonly used is more limited. Other tenses, such as the simple present or imperfect, can be used in their place.

The progressive formation in Portugal consists of the appropriate tense of the verb *estar* ("to be") + *a* + the infinitive of the main verb.

In Brazil, the formation is *estar* + the gerund. The gerund is a verb form that corresponds to the *-ing* form in English. It is formed by adding the following endings to the stem:

-ar Verbs	-er Verbs	-ir Verbs
-ando	-endo	-indo
falar > **falando,** speaking	**comer** > **comendo,** eating	**partir** > **partindo,** leaving

Note: The gerund of *pôr* is *pondo*.

Present Progressive

falar
I am speaking, you are speaking, etc.

estou a falar/estou falando	**estamos a falar/estamos fal**ando
estás a falar/estás falando	**estais a falar/estais fal**ando
está a falar /está falando	**estão a falar/ estão fal**ando

Estou a falar **com a menina.**	I'm speaking to the girl.
O João *está a comer* **o jantar.**	John is eating his dinner.
Vocês *estão escutando***?**	Are you listening?

Imperfect Progressive

comer
I was speaking, you were speaking, etc.

estava a comer/estava comendo	**estávamos a comer/estávamos com**endo
estavas a comer/estavas comendo	**estáveis a comer/estáveis com**endo
estava a comer/estava comendo	**estavam a comer/estavam com**endo

A Maria *estava a comer* **o almoço quando o Pedro chegou.**	Mary was eating lunch when Peter arrived.
Estavas dormindo?	Were you sleeping?
Não *estávamos a fazer* **nada quando o policial nos repreendeu.**	We were not doing anything when the police officer reprimanded us.

Theoretically, a progressive form can be made with any of the tenses, but in practice it is used little, apart from the present, imperfect, and preterite (*estive a falar,* etc.).

Other auxiliary verbs used to express a progressive action are *continuar* ("to continue"), *seguir* ("to follow"; "to go on"), *ficar* ("to stay," "to remain"; "to continue"), especially in Brazil.

Ela *continua a* **mentir.**	She continues to lie.
Ficámos **falando a noite inteira.**	We kept on talking all night long.
O José *seguia* **esperando até meia-noite.**	Joe went on waiting until midnight.

Synopsis of Progressive Tenses

falar—eu

Present Progressive	**estou a falar/falando**	I am speaking
Imperfect Progressive	**estava a falar/falando**	I was speaking
Preterite Progressive	**estive a falar/falando**	I was speaking
Simple Pluperfect Progressive	**estivera a falar/falando**	I had been speaking
Future Progressive	**estarei a falar/falando**	I will be speaking
Conditional Progressive	**estaria a falar/falando**	I would be speaking
Present Perfect	**tenho estado a falar/falando**	I have been speaking
Pluperfect (Past Perfect)	**tinha estado a falar/falando**	I had been speaking
Future Perfect	**terei estado a falar/falando**	I will have been speaking
Conditional Perfect	**teria estado a falar/falando**	I would have been speaking

Keep in mind that in practice, particularly in the spoken language, very few of these forms are used.

5. Reflexive Verbs

A reflexive verb is one where the subject and object of the action are the same person or thing. Thus, the subject acts upon itself. To express this, the verb is always used with a reflexive pronoun. The dictionary will indicate whether a verb is reflexive or not by adding the pronoun -se ("self") after it.

sentar-se, to sit (oneself) down
Present Tense   I sit (myself) down, you sit (yourself) down, etc.

sento-*me*	sentamo-*nos**
sentas-*te*	sentais-*vos*
senta-*se*	sentam-*se*

Sento-me **na cadeira.**   I sit down in the chair.

lavar-se, to wash oneself
Preterite Tense   I washed myself, you washed yourself, etc.

lavei-*me*	lavámo-*nos**
lavaste-*te*	lavastes-*vos*
lavou-*se*	lavaram-*se*

*Note that the *s* is dropped from the verb form of the first person plural when the reflexive pronoun follows the verb.

Lavaste-te **bem?**   Did you wash (yourself) well?
Lavámo-nos **no rio.**   We washed ourselves in the river.

Position of the Reflexive Pronoun

In Portugal, the normal position of the reflexive pronoun is after the verb, joined to it by a hyphen. In Brazil, the reflexive pronoun commonly appears before the verb. In both countries, the pronoun precedes the verb in negative statements, questions, and other circumstances detailed in Chapter 22.

Ela não *se* **lava.**   She does not wash herself.
Nós levantamo-*nos* **cedo.**   We get up early.
Ele não *se sentou* **antes de mim.**   He did not sit down before me.
Como *te* **chamas?**   What's your name? (Literally,
                                                            "What do you call yourself?")

Although some verbs, like *atrever-se,* are always reflexive, others serve a dual purpose, depending on whether they are used with the reflexive pronoun or not.

chamar	to call	**chamar-se**	to be called, to be named
cortar	to cut	**cortar-se**	to cut oneself
deitar	to lay down, to put down	**deitar-se**	to lie down, to go to bed
lavar	to wash	**lavar-se**	to wash oneself
levantar	to lift up, to raise	**levantar-se**	to get up, to rise
sentir	to sense; to suffer	**sentir-se**	to feel; to consider oneself

Reciprocity

The reflexive pronoun may also be used when there is a reciprocal interaction between subjects of a plural verb. The subjects carry out the action on each other.

Vemo-*nos* todos os dias.   We see each other every day.

Sometimes, ambiguity about the true meaning, reflexive or reciprocal, may emerge, such as in:

Felicitaram-*se*. { They congratulated themselves.
{ They congratulated each other.

In order to avoid this problem, the following additions may be useful.

um ao outro/uma à outra }
uns aos outros/umas às outras } (to) one another, each other

mutuamente mutually

Felicitaram-se *um ao outro.* They congratulated each other.
Bateram-se *mutuamente.* They hit each other.

6. Formation of the Subjunctive

Up to now we have concerned ourselves with verb formations in the indicative mood.

The subjunctive mood is another set of tenses, used in such circumstances as giving commands; expressing desire, hope, and volition; after certain conjunctions or expressions; and in general, whenever situations described appear to be doubtful or uncertain.

It is not surprising that many learners throw up their hands in horror at the sheer mention of the word "subjunctive." Having spent precious hours mastering one set of verb endings, it is frustrating to be presented with a completely new set. But, with practice, students can learn to detect when a subjunctive is called for. Paying attention to the subjunctive while reading, to see how and when it is used, can be an especially helpful practice.

The formation of the subjunctive is given first; then, in the next chapter, the occasions when it should be used are described.

Tenses of the Subjunctive

1. Present Subjunctive   *Presente do conjuntivo (subjuntivo—Br.)*
2. Imperfect Subjunctive   *Pretérito imperfeito do conjuntivo*
3. Future Subjunctive   *Futuro do conjuntivo*
4. Present Perfect Subjunctive   *Pretérito perfeito do conjuntivo*
5. Pluperfect (Past Perfect) Subjunctive   *Pretérito mais-que-perfeito do conjuntivo*
6. Future Perfect Subjunctive   *Futuro composto do conjuntivo*

Present Subjunctive

With the exception of the irregular verbs *dar, estar, ser, ir, haver, saber,* and *querer* (see Chapter 8 for forms), all other verbs form the present subjunctive in the same way. The stem is that of the *first person singular of the present indicative,* and the following endings are added:

falar
I (may) speak, you (may) speak, etc.
First person singular (Present Indicative): **fal***o*

Present Subjunctive
fal*e*	**fal***emos*
fal*es*	**fal***eis*
fal*e*	**fal***em*

comer
I (may) eat, you (may) eat, etc.
First person singular (Present Indicative): **com***o*

Present Subjunctive
com*a*	**com***amos*
com*as*	**com***ais*
com*a*	**com***am*

partir
I (may) leave, you (may) leave, etc.
First person singular (Present Indicative): **part***o*

Present Subjunctive
part*a*	**part***amos*
part*as*	**part***ais*
part*a*	**part***am*

In the above examples of regular verbs, the stem used happens to be the same as the normal infinitive stem. However, if we see a verb such as *pedir* ("to ask for"), the infinitive stem is *ped-,* but the first person singular of the present indicative is *peço.* Consequently, the present subjunctive becomes:

pedir
I (may) ask, you (may) ask, etc.
First person singular (Present Indicative): **peç***o*

Present Subjunctive
peç*a*	**peç***amos*
peç*as*	**peç***ais*
peç*a*	**peç***am*

This illustrates the importance of using the stem of the first person singular (present indicative), instead of relying on that of the infinitive.

Notice that the vowels used in the endings of the present subjunctive are the reverse of the indicative mood, as seen in the following third person singular examples.

	Present Indicative	Present Subjunctive
-ar Verbs	**fal***a*	**fal***e*
-er Verbs	**com***e*	**com***a*
-ir Verbs	**part***e*	**part***a*

The next chapter will deal more fully with the uses of the subjunctive. Following are several examples in the present subjunctive.

Espero que *tenham* **boas férias.**	I hope that you have a good vacation.
Talvez ela *venda* **o carro.**	Maybe she'll sell the car.
Preferes que o *faça* **eu?**	Would you rather I do it?
Queremos que o Pedro *trabalhe* **bem.**	We want Peter to work well.
Gosto dela, embora não *goste* **da sua filha.**	I like her, although I don't like her daughter.

Imperfect Subjunctive

The imperfect subjunctive is formed by adding the following endings onto the stem of the *third person plural of the preterite indicative*. Again, following this rule is particularly important where irregular verbs are concerned.

falar
I might, should speak; (if) I spoke, etc.
Third person plural (Preterite Indicative): **fal***aram*

Imperfect Subjunctive

fal*asse*	**fal***ássemos*
fal*asses*	**fal***ásseis*
fal*asse*	**fal***assem*

comer
I might, should eat; (if) I ate, etc.
Third person plural (Preterite Indicative): **com***eram*

Imperfect Subjunctive

com*esse*	**com***éssemos*
com*esses*	**com***ésseis*
com*esse*	**com***essem*

partir
I might, should leave; (if) I left, etc.
Third person plural (Preterite Indicative): **part***iram*

Imperfect Subjunctive

part*isse*	**part***íssemos*
part*isses*	**part***ísseis*
part*isse*	**part***issem*

Like the present subjunctive, there are a number of uses for the imperfect tense, which will be dealt with more fully later.

A Maria lhe pediu que o *fizesse*.	Mary asked him to do it.
Mandaram-me que *partisse* **amanhã.**	They ordered me to leave tomorrow.
Se *comprássemos* **o carro, não teríamos de andar.**	If we bought the car, we would not need to walk.
Embora o Fernando *gostasse* **da Elba, não queria casar-se com ela.**	Although Ferdinand liked Elba, he didn't want to marry her.
Se eu *tivesse* **muito dinheiro, comprava uma casa nova.**	If I had a lot of money, I would buy a new house.

Future Subjunctive

The future subjunctive is also based on the stem of the *third person plural of the preterite indicative,* onto which are added the following endings:

falar
(when, if) I speak, etc.
Third person plural (Preterite Indicative): **fal***aram*

Future Subjunctive

fal*ar*	**fal***armos*
fal*ares*	**fal***ardes*
fal*ar*	**fal***arem*

comer
(when) I eat, etc.
Third person plural (Preterite Indicative): **com***eram*

Future Subjunctive

com*er*	**com***ermos*
com*eres*	**com***erdes*
com*er*	**com***erem*

partir
(when) I leave, etc.
Third person plural (Preterite Indicative): **part***iram*

Future Subjunctive

part*ir*	**part***irmos*
part*ires*	**part***irdes*
part*ir*	**part***irem*

The future subjunctive is used when referring to indefinite or hypothetical future situations. In this context, it often follows such conjunctions as *quando* ("when"), *assim que* ("as soon as"), *se* ("if"), *logo que* ("as soon as"), *conforme* ("depending on whether"), and *enquanto* ("while"), among others.

Quando ela *chegar,* **nós estaremos em Londres.**	When she arrives, we will be in London.
Enquanto a Júlia *for* **à loja, eu faço o jantar.**	While Julia goes to the store, I'll make dinner.
Vamos de férias assim que *tivermos* **o dinheiro.**	We're going on vacation as soon as we have the money.
Se *vir* **o meu irmão, diga-lhe que volte a casa.**	If you see my brother, tell him to come back home.
Faça como *quiser.*	Do as you like.

Present Perfect Subjunctive

The present perfect subjunctive is formed by the present subjunctive of the verb *ter*, plus the past participle of the main verb.

falar
I (may) have spoken, etc.

Present Perfect Subjunctive

tenh*a* **falado**	**tenh***amos* **falado**
tenh*as* **falado**	**tenh***ais* **falado**
tenh*a* **falado**	**tenh***am* **falado**

Duvido que *tenhas feito* **o trabalho.**	I doubt that you have done the work.
É estranho que o menino não *tenha vindo* **à escola.**	It's strange that the boy has not been coming to school.
Talvez não *tenhamos escrito* **o suficiente.**	Perhaps we have not written enough.

Pluperfect (Past Perfect) Subjunctive

The pluperfect subjunctive is formed by the imperfect subjunctive of the verb *ter,* plus the past participle of the main verb.

comer
I might, should have spoken; (if) I had spoken, etc.

Pluperfect Subjunctive

tiv*esse* **comido**	tiv*éssemos* **comido**
tiv*esses* **comido**	tiv*ésseis* **comido**
tiv*esse* **comido**	tiv*essem* **comido**

Se ele *tivesse comido* **o almoço, não teria ficado com fome.**	If he had eaten lunch, he would not have gotten hungry.
O Sr. Mendes fechou a porta, embora a esposa dele a *tivesse aberto.*	Mr. Mendes closed the door, although his wife had opened it.
Achávamos incrível que eles *tivessem gasto* **tanto dinheiro.**	We thought it was incredible that they had spent so much money.

Future Perfect Subjunctive

The future perfect subjunctive is formed by the future subjunctive of the verb *ter,* plus the past participle of the main verb.

partir
(when, if) I have left, etc.

tiv*er* **partido**	tiv*ermos* **partido**
tiv*eres* **partido**	tiv*erdes* **partido**
tiv*er* **partido**	tiv*erem* **partido**

Se *tiveres comido* **tudo, sairemos.**	If you have eaten it all, we'll go out.
Quando a Maria *tiver terminado* **a limpeza, vai tomar um café.**	When Mary has finished the cleaning, she's going to have coffee.
Assim que *tivermos chegado,* **visitaremos o museu.**	As soon as we have arrived, we will visit the museum.

Checklist of Endings

Subjunctive Tenses

	-ar		**-er**		**-ir**	
Present	-e	-emos	-a	-amos	-a	-amos
	-es	-eis	-as	-ais	-as	-ais
	-e	-em	-a	-am	-a	-am
Imperfect	-asse	-ássemos	-esse	-éssemos	-isse	-íssemos
	-asses	-ásseis	-esses	-ésseis	-isses	-ísseis
	-asse	-assem	-esse	-essem	-isse	-issem
Future	-ar	-armos	-er	-ermos	-ir	-irmos
	-ares	-ardes	-eres	-erdes	-ires	-irdes
	-ar	-arem	-er	-erem	-ir	-irem

Present Perfect   *ter* + past participle

tenha _____	tenhamos _____
tenhas _____	tenhais _____
tenha _____	tenham _____

Pluperfect   *ter* + past participle
(Past Perfect)

tivesse _____	tivéssemos _____
tivesses _____	tivésseis _____
tivesse _____	tivessem _____

Future Perfect   *ter* + past participle

tiver _____	tivermos _____
tiveres _____	tiverdes _____
tiver _____	tiverem _____

Synopsis of Subjunctive Tenses

falar—eu

Present	**fale**	I may speak
Imperfect	**falasse**	I might, should speak; (if) I spoke
Future	**falar**	(when, if) I speak
Present Perfect	**tenha falado**	I may have spoken
Pluperfect (Past Perfect)	**tivesse falado**	Might, should I have spoken; (if) I had spoken
Future Perfect	**tiver falado**	(when, if) I have spoken

7. Uses of the Subjunctive

The subjunctive mood of verbs is used, generally speaking, when the situation concerned is only a possibility and not yet a fact at the moment it is being spoken or
written about. It encompasses a wide range of conditions dealing with behavior and
emotions toward other people, remote and doubtful circumstances, and uncertainty.
The following is a list of the aspects of the subjunctive discussed in this chapter:

1. Commands
2. Verbs Expressing Desire, Doubt, and Volition
3. Verbs Expressing Emotion
4. Impersonal Verbs
5. Conjunctions and Related Expressions
6. Indefinite Antecedents
7. Special Expressions
8. Conditional Sentences

Commands

The command form, or *imperative,* is discussed in detail in Chapter 13. The present
subjunctive is used for both affirmative and negative commands with *você* and *vocês*.
With *tu,* it is used only in the negative.

(você)	*Fale* **mais alto!**	Speak louder!
(vocês)	*Comam* **os legumes!**	Eat your vegetables!
(tu)	**Não** *compres* **o vestido!**	Don't buy the dress!
(você)	**Não me** *olhe***!**	Don't look at me!

Command Verbs

dizer	to tell
mandar	to order, to tell
ordenar	to order

Ordeno-lhe *que abra* **a porta.**	I order you to open the door.
Mandou-lhes *que saíssem* **do carro.**	He ordered them to get out of the car.
Maria lhe disse *que fosse* **embora.**	Mary told him to go away.

Note the use of the indirect object pronouns in these examples. With *mandar* and
dizer, the infinitive can also be used.

Mando-os *sairem* **do carro.**	I'm telling you to get out of the car.

Verbs Expressing Desire, Doubt, and Volition

The subjunctive is also used after verbs that fall into this category. The verb in the subordinate clause (that part of the sentence that generally follows the word *que* ["that"]) is in the subjunctive.

não admitir	not to allow
aconselhar	to advise
consentir	to consent to
desejar	to want, to desire
duvidar	to doubt
esperar	to hope, to wish
implorar	to implore, to beg
negar	to deny
pedir	to ask for
persuadir	to persuade
precisar	to need
preferir	to prefer
proibir	to forbid

Espero *que tenha* **boas notícias.**
I hope that you have good news.

Eles não admitiam *que* **o filho** *saísse* **tarde à noite.**
They did not allow their son to go out late at night.

Eu preferia *que o fizesses* **tu.**
I would prefer that you do it.

Vamos proibir *que* **os rapazes** *joguem* **futebol na rua.**
We're going to forbid the boys from playing soccer in the street.

Implorei ao professor *que* **me** *desse* **boas notas.**
I begged the teacher to give me good grades.

Note: If the subject of the verb expressing desire, doubt, or volition is the same as that of the second verb, the infinitive construction is used.

Espero *fazer* **uma bela visita a Roma.**   I hope to take a wonderful trip to Rome.

Verbs Expressing Emotion

alegrar-se	to be glad
estranhar	to be surprised
sentir	to feel; to feel sorry
ter medo	to be frightened
ter pena	to be sorry (for)

Sinto muito que a tua mãe *esteja* **doente.**	I'm very sorry that your mother is ill.
Ela tinha medo que o Miguel não *voltasse* **são e salvo.**	She was afraid that Michael wouldn't return home safe and sound.
Estranhamos que ela *deixe* **os filhos sozinhos na casa.**	We are surprised that she leaves her children all alone in the house.

Impersonal Verbs

The subjunctive is used after expressions called *impersonal verbs*; in English, these expressions usually begin with "it."

Impersonal Expressions

é estranho	it is strange
é incrível	it is incredible
é lógico	it is logical
é natural	it is natural
é possível	it is possible
é provável	it is probable

É provável que a minha tia *venha* **visitar-nos hoje.**	It is possible that my aunt is coming to visit us today.
Era estranho que os cães *tivessem* **feito tanto barulho.**	It was strange that the dogs had made so much noise.

However, the following expressions, indicating true or clear-cut situations, are in the *indicative mood,* except when used in the negative, as contrary to fact.

é certo	it is true; it is certain
é evidente	it is evident
é manifesto	it is clear
é óbvio	it is obvious
é verdade	it is true

É verdade que ela *vai* **para Itália.**	It is true that she's going to Italy.
Não era certo que o time *fosse* **ganhar o troféu.**	It wasn't certain that the team was going to win the trophy.

Impersonal expressions can also be used with the infinitive, if the dependent verb has no definite subject.

É possível *ganhar* **milhões na loteria.**	It's possible to win millions in the lottery.
Não é natural *falar* **dessa maneira.**	It's not natural to speak that way.

Conjunctions and Related Expressions

There are a variety of conjunctions (words that join parts of sentences together) and other similar expressions that are followed by a verb in the subjunctive.

a fim de que	in order that	**contanto que**	provided that
a não ser que	unless	**embora**	although
ainda quando	even if	**mesmo que**	even if
ainda que	although	**para que**	in order that
ainda se	even if	**posto que**	although
antes que	before	**primeiro que**	before
até que	until	**se bem que**	although
(no) caso que	in the case that	**sem que**	without
conquanto	although	**sob condição que**	on condition that

Ainda que o *diga* **cem vezes, nunca me escuta.**	Even if I say it a hundred times, he never listens to me.
Vou comprar o anel *posto que custe* **muito dinheiro.**	I'm going to buy the ring, even though it costs a lot.
Deixei o João vir conosco *sob condição que ficasse* **calado.**	I let John come with us on condition that he kept quiet.
Esconde esta mala *antes que chegue* **ao porto.**	Hide this suitcase before you get to the port.
Vou preparar o jantar *a não ser que queiras* **jantar fora.**	I'm going to make dinner unless you want to dine out.

Talvez, Oxalá, and *Tomara que*

The subjunctive is used after the adverb *talvez* ("perhaps," "maybe") and the interjections *oxalá* and *tomara que* (Br.) ("God willing"; "hopefully").

Talvez **ela** *venha* **logo.**	Perhaps she will come soon.
Oxalá **não** *chova* **no piquenique.**	Let's hope it doesn't rain on the picnic.
Tomara que **eles falem português.**	Hopefully, they speak Portuguese.

Hypothetical Expressions

como quer que	however
onde quer que	wherever
por mais que	however much
por muito(s) que	however much (many)
quem quer que	whoever

The above expressions also call for the subjunctive.

Onde quer que haja **gente, há também poluição.**	Wherever people are, pollution is there too.
Como quer que **se** *veja* **o problema, não há solução.**	However you look at the problem, there's no solution.
Por mais que estudes, **não podes aprender tudo.**	However much you study, you cannot learn it all.
Não vou poder comprá-lo, *por muitos* **dólares** *que tenha.*	No matter how many dollars I have, I won't be able to buy it.

Indefinite Antecedents

In relative clauses (those that refer back to the main part of the sentence) introduced by *que*, the subjunctive is used when there is no definite or specific antecedent (the person or thing immediately preceding *que*).

Tem *uma blusa* **que me** *sirva*?	Do you have a blouse that would fit me?
Procuramos *alguém* **que** *fale* **alemão.**	We are looking for someone who speaks German.
Conheces *alguma pessoa* **que** *possa* **pintar bem a nossa casa?**	Do you know anyone who could paint our house?

Compare with these sentences describing definite situations:

Tem a blusa que me serve?	Do you have the blouse that fits me?
Conhecemos alguém que fala dez línguas.	We know somebody who speaks ten languages.

These examples refer to established facts.

Special Expressions

These special expressions employ both the present and future subjunctive:

seja o que for	whatever it may be
seja como for	however it may be
seja quanto for	however much it may be
seja quando for	whenever it may be
esteja onde estiver	wherever he, she, or it may be
venha o que vier	come what may
custe o que custar	at whatever cost

This construction can be applied to many other verbs.

It can also be used to describe past circumstances and events, with both verbs in the imperfect subjunctive.

fosse o que fosse   whatever it might be
estivesse onde estivesse   wherever he, she, or it might be

Conditional Sentences

The subjunctive is used in sentences containing a clause introduced by *se* ("if"), when stating a possibility that is doubtful or contrary to fact. These are known as conditional sentences, because the word *se* imposes a condition upon the action.

Se tivesse **dinheiro, poderia lhe**   If I had money, I could buy you a nice
  comprar um presente bonito.   present.
Se não tivesses **gasto tudo, podias ter**   If you hadn't spent everything, you
  comprado o livro.   could have bought the book.
Se pudesse **contactá-lo, ficaria mais**   If I could contact him, I would feel
  aliviada.   more relieved.

Observe that when the conditional sentence states a likelihood or certainty, the main clause remains in the indicative.

Se tiverem **tempo,** *visitarão* **o castelo.**   If they have the time, they will visit
                                                        the castle.

8. Irregular Verbs

Only the irregular tenses are given; the remaining tenses of these verbs are regular.

dar to give *dando* *dado*

Pres.	**dou, dás, dá,** damos, dais, **dão**
Pret.	**dei, deste, deu, demos, destes, deram**
Simple Plup.	**dera, deras, dera, déramos, déreis, deram**
Pres. Subj.	**dê, dês, dê,** demos, deis, **dêem**
Imp. Subj.	**desse, desses, desse, déssemos, désseis, dessem**
Fut. Subj.	**der, deres, der, dermos, derdes, derem**

dizer to say *dizendo* *dito*

Pres.	**digo,** dizes, **diz,** dizemos, dizeis, dizem
Pret.	**disse, disseste, disse, dissemos, dissestes, disseram**
Simple Plup.	**dissera, disseras, dissera, disséramos, disséreis, disseram**
Fut.	**direi, dirás, dirá, diremos, direis, dirão**
Condit.	**diria, dirias, diria, diríamos, diríeis, diriam**

estar to be *estando* *estado*

Pres.	**estou, estás, está,** estamos, estais, **estão**
Pret.	**estive, estiveste, esteve, estivemos, estivestes, estiveram**
Simple Plup.	**estivera, estiveras, estivera, estivéramos, estivéreis, estiveram**
Pres. Subj.	**esteja, estejas, esteja, estejamos, estejais, estejam**
Imp. Subj.	**estivesse, estivesses, estivesse, estivéssemos, estivésseis, estivessem**
Fut. Subj.	**estiver, estiveres, estiver, estivermos, estiverdes, estiverem**

fazer to do; to make *fazendo* *feito*

Pres.	**faço,** fazes, **faz,** fazemos, fazeis, fazem
Pret.	**fiz, fizeste, fez, fizemos, fizestes, fizeram**
Simple Plup.	**fizera, fizeras, fizera, fizéramos, fizéreis, fizeram**
Fut.	**farei, farás, fará, faremos, fareis, farão**
Condit.	**faria, farias, faria, faríamos, faríeis, fariam**
Pres. Subj.	**faça, faças, faça, façamos, façais, façam**
Imp. Subj.	**fizesse, fizesses, fizesse, fizéssemos, fizésseis, fizessem**
Fut. Subj.	**fizer, fizeres, fizer, fizermos, fizerdes, fizerem**

haver   to have   *havendo*   *havido*

Pres.	**hei, hás, há,** havemos, haveis, **hão**
Pret.	**houve, houveste, houve, houvemos, houvestes, houveram**
Simple Plup.	**houvera, houveras, houvera, houvéramos, houvéreis, houveram**
Pres. Subj.	**haja, hajas, haja, hajamos, hajais, hajam**
Imp. Subj.	**houvesse, houvesses, houvesse, houvéssemos, houvésseis, houvessem**
Fut. Subj.	**houver, houveres, houver, houvermos, houverdes, houverem**

ir   to go   *indo*   *ido*

Pres.	**vou, vais, vai, vamos, ides, vão**
Pret.	**fui, foste, foi, fomos, fostes, foram**
Simple Plup.	**fora, foras, fora, fôramos, fôreis, foram**
Pres. Subj.	**vá, vás, vá, vamos, vades, vão**
Imp. Subj.	**fosse, fosses, fosse, fôssemos, fôsseis, fossem**
Fut. Subj.	**for, fores, for, formos, fordes, forem**

poder   to be able, can   *podendo*   *podido*

Pres.	**posso,** podes, pode, podemos, podeis, podem
Pret.	**pude, pudeste, pôde, pudemos, pudestes, puderam**
Simple Plup.	**pudera, puderas, pudera, pudéramos, pudéreis, puderam**
Pres. Subj.	**possa, possas, possa, possamos, possais, possam**
Imp. Subj.	**pudesse, pudesses, pudesse, pudéssemos, pudésseis, pudessem**
Fut. Subj.	**puder, puderes, puder, pudermos, puderdes, puderem**

pôr   to put   *pondo*   *posto*

Pres.	**ponho, pões, põe, pomos, pondes, põem**
Imperf.	**punha, punhas, punha, púnhamos, púnheis, punham**
Pret.	**pus, puseste, pôs, pusemos, pusestes, puseram**
Simple Plup.	**pusera, puseras, pusera, puséramos, puséreis, puseram**
Pres. Subj.	**ponha, ponhas, ponha, ponhamos, ponhais, ponham**
Imp. Subj.	**pusesse, pusesses, pusesse, puséssemos, pusésseis, pusessem**
Fut. Subj.	**puser, puseres, puser, pusermos, puserdes, puserem**

querer to want to, to wish   *querendo*   *querido*

Pres.	quero, queres, **quer,** queremos, quereis, querem
Pret.	**quis, quiseste, quis, quisemos, quisestes, quiseram**
Simple Plup.	**quisera, quiseras, quisera, quiséramos, quiséreis, quiseram**
Pres. Subj.	**queira, queiras, queira, queiramos, queirais, queiram**
Imp. Subj.	**quisesse, quisesses, quisesse, quiséssemos, quisésseis, quisessem**
Fut. Subj.	**quiser, quiseres, quiser, quisermos, quiserdes, quiserem**

saber to know   *sabendo*   *sabido*

Pres.	**sei,** sabes, sabe, sabemos, sabeis, sabem
Pret.	**soube, soubeste, soube, soubemos, soubestes, souberam**
Simple Plup.	**soubera, souberas, soubera, soubéramos, soubéreis, souberam**
Pres. Subj.	**saiba, saibas, saiba, saibamos, saibais, saibam**
Imp. Subj.	**soubesse, soubesses, soubesse, soubéssemos, soubésseis, soubessem**
Fut. Subj.	**souber, souberes, souber, soubermos, souberdes, souberem**

ser to be   *sendo*   *sido*

Pres.	**sou, és, é, somos, sois, são**
Imperf.	**era, eras, era, éramos, éreis, eram**
Pret.	**fui, foste, foi, fomos, fostes, foram**
Simple Plup.	**fora, foras, fora, fôramos, fôreis, foram**
Pres. Subj.	**seja, sejas, seja, sejamos, sejais, sejam**
Imp. Subj.	**fosse, fosses, fosse, fôssemos, fôsseis, fossem**
Fut. Subj.	**for, fores, for, formos, fordes, forem**

ter to have   *tendo*   *tido*

Pres.	**tenho, tens, tem,** temos, **tendes, têm**
Imperf.	**tinha, tinhas, tinha, tínhamos, tínheis, tinham**
Pret.	**tive, tiveste, teve, tivemos, tivestes, tiveram**
Simple Plup.	**tivera, tiveras, tivera, tivéramos, tivéreis, tiveram**
Pres. Subj.	**tenha, tenhas, tenha, tenhamos, tenhais, tenham**
Imp. Subj.	**tivesse, tivesses, tivesse, tivéssemos, tivésseis, tivessem**
Fut. Subj.	**tiver, tiveres, tiver, tivermos, tiverdes, tiverem**

trazer   to bring   *trazendo*   *trazido*

Pres.	**trago,** trazes, **traz,** trazemos, trazeis, trazem
Pret.	**trouxe, trouxeste, trouxe, trouxemos, trouxestes, trouxeram**
Simple Plup.	**trouxera, trouxeras, trouxera, trouxéramos, trouxéreis, trouxeram**
Fut.	**trarei, trarás, trará, traremos, trareis, trarão**
Condit.	**traria, trarias, traria, traríamos, traríeis, trariam**
Pres. Subj.	**traga, tragas, traga, tragamos, tragais, tragam**
Imp. Subj.	**trouxesse, trouxesses, trouxesse, trouxéssemos, trouxésseis, trouxessem**
Fut. Subj.	**trouxer, trouxeres, trouxer, trouxermos, trouxerdes, trouxerem**

ver   to see   *vendo*   *visto*

Pres.	**vejo, vês, vê,** vemos, **vedes, vêem**
Pret.	vi, **viste, viu, vimos, vistes, viram**
Simple Plup.	**vira, viras, vira, víramos, víreis, viram**
Pres. Subj.	**veja, vejas, veja, vejamos, vejais, vejam**
Imp. Subj.	**visse, visses, visse, víssemos, vísseis, vissem**
Fut. Subj.	**vir, vires, vir, virmos, virdes, virem**

vir   to come   *vindo*   *vindo*

Pres.	**venho, vens, vem,** vimos, **vindes, vêm**
Imperf.	**vinha, vinhas, vinha, vínhamos, vínheis, vinham**
Pret.	**vim, vieste, veio, viemos, viestes, vieram**
Simple Plup.	**viera, vieras, viera, viéramos, viéreis, vieram**
Pres. Subj.	**venha, venhas, venha, venhamos, venhais, venham**
Imp. Subj.	**viesse, viesses, viesse, viéssemos, viésseis, viessem**
Fut. Subj.	**vier, vieres, vier, viermos, vierdes, vierem**

The following verbs are irregular in the first person singular, and therefore the present subjunctives are also irregular:

crer   to believe   *crendo*   *crido*

Pres.	**creio, crês, crê,** cremos, **credes, crêem**
Pres. Subj.	**creia, creias, creia, creiamos, creiais, creiam**

ler   to read   *lendo*   *lido*

Pres.	**leio, lês, lê,** lemos, **ledes, lêem**
Pres. Subj.	**leia, leias, leia, leiamos, leiais, leiam**

medir   to measure   *medindo*   *medido*

Pres.   **meço,** medes, mede, medimos, medis, medem
Pres. Subj.   **meça, meças, meça, meçamos, meçais, meçam**

ouvir   to hear   *ouvindo*   *ouvido*

Pres.   **ouço,** ouves, ouve, ouvimos, ouvis, ouvem
Pres. Subj.   **ouça, ouças, ouça, ouçamos, ouçais, ouçam**

pedir   to ask for   *pedindo*   *pedido*

Pres.   **peço,** pedes, pede, pedimos, pedis, pedem
Pres. Subj.   **peça, peças, peça, peçamos, peçais, peçam**

perder   to lose   *perdendo*   *perdido*

Pres.   **perco,** perdes, perde, perdemos, perdeis, perdem
Pres. Subj.   **perca, percas, perca, percamos, percais, percam**

rir   to laugh   *rindo*   *rido*

Pres.   **rio, ris, ri,** rimos, **rides, riem**
Pres. Subj.   **ria, rias, ria, riamos, riais, riam**

valer   to be worth   *valendo*   *valido*

Pres.   **valho,** vales, vale, valemos, valeis, valem
Pres. Subj.   **valha, valhas, valha, valhamos, valhais, valham**

9. *Ser, Estar,* and *Ficar*

In Portuguese, there is more than one way of expressing the verb "to be" ("I am," "you are," "he is," etc.), and the three verbs above can be used to fulfil this function, each in specific circumstances. The full conjugations of the verbs were given in Chapter 8; the present tense is listed here as a reminder.

	ser	*estar*	*ficar*
eu	**sou**	**estou**	**fico**
tu	**és**	**estás**	**ficas**
ele, ela, você	**é**	**está**	**fica**
nós	**somos**	**estamos**	**ficamos**
vós	**sois**	**estais**	**ficais**
eles, elas, vocês	**são**	**estão**	**ficam**

Ficar is regular, except for certain spelling changes (see Chapter 12).

Ser

1. To express inherent or permanent characteristics of people, places, and things (nationality, size, color, appearance, composition, marital status, profession, etc.)

A Maria *é* **uma advogada trabalhadora.**
Mary is a hardworking lawyer.

Eu? *Sou* **alemão, mas moro em Portugal.**
Me? I'm German, but I live in Portugal.

Eles *são* **muito ricos.**
They're very rich.

2. To denote origin and possession

De onde *é*? *Sou* **de Chicago.**
Where are you from? I'm from Chicago.

Esta mesa *é* **de Macau.**
This table is from Macau.

De quem *são* **estes livros?**
Whose books are these?

São **da Lídia.**
They belong to Lidia.

3. To tell time. *Ser* is used exclusively with expressions of time.

Que horas *são*?
What time is it?

São **duas e meia.**
It's two-thirty.

É **meia-noite.**
It's midnight.

4. To describe permanent location. Used for geographic areas, places, and objects in a fixed position (buildings, landmarks, parks, etc.)

Onde *é* **o Banco do Brasil?**   Where is the Bank of Brazil?
O Brasil *é* **na América do Sul.**   Brazil is in South America.

5. To form impersonal expressions

É **impossível.**   It's impossible.
É **preciso.**   It's necessary.

6. To form passive sentences, together with a past participle (see Chapter 14)

O rato *foi morto* **pelo gato.**   The rat was killed by the cat.
A loteria *foi ganha* **por uma**   The lottery was won by a little old lady.
velhinha.

7. To describe weather, when referring to an inherent characteristic of climate

No equador *é* **sempre quente.**   It's always hot on the equator.
Antigamente, *era* **sempre frio na**   It used to always be cold in
Escandinávia, mas hoje em dia   Scandinavia, but these days it's
é **mais razoável.**   milder.

For temporary conditions, however, it is more common to use other verbs for weather, such as *fazer, haver,* and *estar.*

Faz **frio.**   It's cold.
Há **calor.**   It's hot.
Estava **quente demais.**   It was too hot.

Estar

Estar is used for situations of change, movement, and temporary circumstances.

1. To express temporary or variable states, including moods, health, and other conditions subject to change

Como *está*? *Estou* **bem, obrigado.**   How are you? I'm well, thanks.
Ela *está* **muito cansada hoje.**   She is very tired today.
A porta *está* **fechada.**   The door is closed.
A sopa *estava* **fria quando chegou**   The soup was cold by the time it arrived
à mesa.   at the table.
Esta laranja não *está* **boa.**   This orange is no good.

2. To express temporary position or location

Onde *está* **o carro?**	Where is the car?
O livro *está* **debaixo da mesa.**	The book is under the table.
Os senhores Silva *estão* **em Berlim.**	Mr. and Mrs. Silva are in Berlin.
Agora, onde *estará* **a minha carteira?**	Now then, where can my purse be?

3. To describe the weather, when referring to a temporary climatic state

Hoje *está* **muito quente.**	It's very hot today.
O ano passado *estava* **tão frio que não saímos.**	Last year it was so cold that we did not go out.

4. To form the progressive tenses (see Chapter 4)

Estou a brincar **com o meu gato.**	I'm playing with my cat.
Eles *estavam a correr* **quando o Pedro escorregou.**	They were running when Peter slipped.
Ela *está fazendo* **barulho.**	She is making noise.

5. To take the place of *ter* in the expression *estar + com* (see Chapter 10)

Estamos com **sono.**	We are sleepy.
Está com **sede.**	He is thirsty.
Estava com **fome.**	She was hungry.

Ficar

1. To take the place of *ser*, when used in reference to permanent locations

Onde *fica* **a farmácia?**	Where is the pharmacy?
Onde *fica* **o museu?**	Where is the museum?
A praia *fica* **muito longe.**	The beach is a long way off.

2. To describe a changed state, emotion, or condition

Ela *ficou* **zangada comigo.**	She became angry with me.
O meu pai sempre *fica* **feliz quando está no jardim.**	My father is always happy when he is in the garden.
O céu *ficou* **escuro e começou a chover.**	The sky became dark and it began to rain.

3. To express judgment on suitability, fit, or appropriateness

A blusa *fica-lhe* **bem.**   The blouse really flatters you.

Aquela atitude dela *ficou muito feia.*   That attitude of hers was very unbecoming.

10. *Ter* and *Haver*

Both of these verbs in Portuguese express "to have," but, depending on the circumstances in which they are used, they can differ in meaning. *Ter* is the more regularly used verb, while *haver* has a more limited function.

	ter	*haver*
eu	**tenho**	**hei**
tu	**tens**	**hás**
ele, ela, você	**tem**	**há**
nós	**temos**	**havemos**
vós	**tendes**	**haveis**
eles, elas, vocês	**têm**	**hão**

Ter

Ter is used in the following situations:

> To express possession
> With ages
> As a substitute for *estar* or *ser*
> To describe a problem or illness.

A Maria *tem* **uma casa bonita.**	Mary has a pretty house.
Quantos anos *tens*? *Tenho* **vinte.**	How old are you? I'm twenty.
Os alpinistas *tinham* **muito frio na montanha.**	The mountain climbers were very cold on the mountain.
O que *tem* **a sua irmã? Ela está sempre triste.**	What's wrong with your sister? She's always sad.

Ter de, *Ter que*

Ter is also used in these expressions, when denoting necessity or obligation.

Não temos carne; vou *ter de* **ir ao talho.**	We have no meat; I'll have to go to the butcher shop.
O Marco *teve que* **sair de negócio.**	Mark had to leave on business.

Ter in Compound Tenses

Ter is used as the auxiliary verb in the perfect tenses.

Ultimamente, a Silvana *tem estudado* **muito.**	Silvana has been studying a lot lately.
Tínhamos partido **antes da tua chegada.**	We had left before your arrival.

Haver

Haver is used in the following situations, primarily in the third person singular:

> To mean "there is," "there are"
> To denote an event
> To describe temporary weather conditions.

Há **um supermercado na praça.**	There is a supermarket in the square.
Não *havia* **nada para fazer.**	There was nothing to do.
Ontem *houve* **um bom programa no rádio.**	Yesterday there was a good program on the radio.
Houve **um acidente na nossa rua.**	There was an accident on our street.
Que barulho! O que é que *há*?	What a racket! What's going on?
Havia **muito sol quando chegámos.**	It was very sunny when we arrived.

Expressions of Time

Haver is used to denote the passage of time (*haver* + unit of time).

Há **muito tempo que estou a esperar.**	I have been waiting for a long time.
Ela partiu *há* **meia hora.**	She left half an hour ago.
Havia **muitos anos que eles não se falavam.**	They had not talked to each other for many years.

Haver de + Infinitive

This construction, although rarely used, denotes strong intention to do something. *De* is joined to the main part of the verb when the verb is monosyllabic *(hei, hás, há, hão)*.

Qualquer dia ele *há-de falar* **chinês bem, ele estuda tanto.**
One day he really will speak Chinese well, he studies so much.

Não tinha dinheiro, o que *havia de fazer*?
I had no money, what on earth could I do?

Hei-de ganhar **a loteria.**
I've got to win the lottery sometime.

Haver in Compound Tenses

The usage of *haver* as an auxiliary verb is rather archaic and usually reserved for highly literary writing styles. It is rarely heard in the spoken language.

A Dona Alícia *haverá partido* **para tomar as águas antes da chegada do Conde de Vila Nova.**

Lady Alice will have departed to take the waters of the spa before the arrival of the Count of Vila Nova.

11. Radical-Changing Verbs

A number of verbs in Portuguese change their spelling slightly in the present indicative tense. The change occurs in the stem, or *radical*, of the verb in all persons except the *nós* and *vós* forms. Since the present subjunctive is based on the first person singular of the present indicative, its correct spelling is a vital starting point for the formation of the present subjunctive.

Following are some of the more common types of radical-changing verbs.

First conjugation, *-ar*

> *boiar*, to float
> **bóio, bóias, bóia,** boiamos, boiais, **bóiam**
> A written accent is added.

> *recear*, to fear
> **receio, receias, receia,** receamos, receais, **receiam**
> An *i* is added.

> *odiar*, to hate
> **odeio, odeias, odeia,** odiamos, odiais, **odeiam**
> An *e* is added.

Second conjugation, *-er*

> *erguer*, to rise
> **ergo,** ergues, ergue, erguemos, ergueis, erguem
> Irregular only in the first person singular.

Third conjugation, *-ir*

The majority of changes occur in these verbs. The changes take place in the first person singular and carry over to the present subjunctive.

The *e* changes to *i*.

Infinitive		Present Indicative	Present Subjunctive
conseguir	to achieve	**cons***i***go**	**cons***i***ga**
divertir	to enjoy	**div***i***rto**	**div***i***rta**
mentir	to lie	**m***i***nto**	**m***i***nta**
repetir	to repeat	**rep***i***to**	**rep***i***ta**
seguir	to follow	**s***i***go**	**s***i***ga**
sentir	to feel	**s***i***nto**	**s***i***nta**
servir	to serve	**s***i***rvo**	**s***i***rva**
vestir	to dress	**v***i***sto**	**v***i***sta**

The *o* changes to *u*.

cobrir	to cover	**c***u***bro**	**c***u***bra**
descobrir	to discover	**desc***u***bro**	**desc***u***bra**
dormir	to sleep	**d***u***rmo**	**d***u***rma**

Here, the change occurs three times.

subir, to go up
subo, **s***o***bes, s***o***be,** subimos, subis, **s***o***bem**

12. Orthographic-Changing Verbs

Orthographic-changing verbs require a slight modification in their spelling (*orthography*) to maintain correct pronunciation. The spelling change takes place in the last consonant of the verb stem before certain vowels, as listed below. The most common changes are as follows:

1. Verbs Ending in *-car*

Before *e* or *i*, the *c* changes to *qu* to maintain the hard *c* sound.

ficar, to stay, to remain
fico I stay   **fiquei** I stayed

Other verbs of this type are:

acercar-se	to approach
brincar	to play
colocar	to place
explicar	to explain
indicar	to indicate
modificar	to modify
multiplicar	to multiply
publicar	to publish
sacar	to remove
tocar	to touch; to play (an instrument)

2. Verbs Ending in *-çar*

Before *e* or *i*, the *ç* changes to *c,* since the cedilla is not required to maintain the soft *c* sound.

caçar, to hunt
caço I hunt   **cacei** I hunted

Other verbs of this type are:

almoçar	to have lunch
ameaçar	to threaten
calçar	to put on shoes
começar	to begin

3. Verbs Ending in *-gar*

Before *e* or *i*, the *g* becomes *gu* to maintain the hard *g* sound.

chegar, to arrive
chego I arrive   **che*gu*ei** I arrived

Other verbs of this type are:

apagar	to extinguish
entregar	to hand over
jogar	to play
julgar	to judge
obrigar	to compel; to oblige
pagar	to pay
prolongar	to prolong

4. Verbs Ending in *-cer*

Before *a* or *o,* the *c* becomes *ç* to maintain the soft *c* sound.

conhecer, to know
conheço I know   **conhece** he knows

Other verbs of this type are:

acontecer	to happen
agradecer	to thank
merecer	to deserve
obedecer	to obey
reconhecer	to recognize

5. Verbs Ending in *-ger* and *-gir*

Before *a* or *o,* the *g* becomes *j* to maintain the soft *g* sound.

fugir, to flee
fu*j*o I flee   **foge** he flees

Other verbs of this type are:

afligir	to afflict; to distress
corrigir	to correct
dirigir	to drive; to direct
exigir	to demand; to require
fingir	to pretend
proteger	to protect

6. Verbs Ending in *-guer* and *-guir*

Before *a* or *o*, *gu* simply becomes *g* to maintain the hard *g* sound.

seguir, to follow
sig**o** I follow   **segue** he follows

Other verbs of this type are:

conseguir	to achieve; to obtain
distinguir	to distinguish
erguer	to erect
perseguir	to pursue; to persecute

13. Commands (Imperatives)

It has already been shown in Chapter 7 that indirect commands, orders, and requests are formed by using the appropriate verb in the subjunctive. (*Mando-lhe que me escreva.* I order him to write me.) The subjunctive is also used for direct commands, both affirmative and negative, in the polite third person forms (*você, vocês; o senhor/a senhora, os senhores/as senhoras*) and for negative commands in the familiar second person forms (*tu, vós*).

Affirmative Commands

1. The *Tu* Form

The command form for *tu* (used with friends, family, young children, people of similar social rank, and pets) is exactly the same verb form as the *third person singular* of the present indicative.

falar	to speak	**fala**
fazer	to do	**faz**
comer	to eat	**come**
partir	to leave	**parte**

Faz a tua cama antes de sair!	Make your bed before you go out!
Toca a campainha ou eles não saem.	Ring the bell or they won't come out.
Escreve a receita antes de te esquecer.	Write down the recipe before you forget.
Entrega os documentos ao senhor Silva.	Hand over the documents to Mr. Silva.
Cobre o bolo para que as moscas não o toquem.	Cover the cake so that the flies don't touch it.

2. The *Vós* Form

The archaic *vós* form is still used in church services, political speeches, and by older people in remote areas.

The command form for *vós* is also based on the present indicative. The final *s* is simply removed from the second person plural form of the verb.

cantar to sing	**cantai**
receber to receive	**recebei**
resistir to resist	**resisti**
ir to go	**ide**

Louvai **ao Senhor.**	Praise the Lord.
Trazei **as almas até o santuário de Deus.**	Bring your souls to God's sanctuary.
Escutai **a palavra do vosso líder.**	Listen to the word of your leader.
Ponde **o chá na mesa, filhas.**	Put the tea on the table, girls.
Fechai **a porta rápido.**	Close the door quickly.

3. The *Você* Form

To command in the *você* form (used with strangers, older people, and those of higher social rank; used exclusively in much of Brazil), the verb goes into the present subjunctive.

dançar to dance	**dance**
escrever to write	**escreva**
insistir to insist	**insista**
dizer to say	**diga**

Durma **sem cobertor ou vai ficar muito quente.**	Sleep without a blanket or you'll get very hot.
Apague **a luz antes da meia-noite.**	Put the light out before midnight.
Diga **o seu nome completo por favor.**	Please say your full name.
Peça **a lista para nós.**	Ask for the menu for us.
Traga **as malas para o táxi.**	Bring the suitcases to the taxi.

4. The *Vocês* Form

As above, the *vocês* form goes into the appropriate present subjunctive.

lavar to wash	**lavem**
beber to drink	**bebam**
cobrir to cover	**cubram**
pôr to put	**ponham**

Chamem **a polícia.**	Call the police.
Contem-me **o que aconteceu.**	Tell me what happened.
Convidem **os senhores Tavares para o churrasco.**	Invite the Tavares to the barbecue.
Fiquem **aqui até chegar o pai.**	Wait here until your father arrives.
Tenham **pena do pobre rapaz.**	Take pity on the poor boy.

Negative Commands

All negative commands use the appropriate present-subjunctive form.

esperar to wait	**não esperes (tu)**
correr to run	**não corrais (vós)**
abrir to open	**não abra (você)**
trazer to bring	**não tragam (vocês)**

Não te sentes **perto de mim.**	Don't sit near me.
Não deiteis **fora os restos do jantar.**	Don't throw out the leftovers from dinner.
Não **lhe** *dê* **o seu coração.**	Don't give him your heart.
Não atravessem **a rua sem ajuda.**	Don't cross the street without help.
Não subas **estas escadas.**	Don't go up these stairs.
Não feche **a loja até a uma.**	Don't close the store until one o'clock.

Polite Commands

Requests can be softened by using the construction *fazer favor de* + infinitive.

Faz favor de abrir **a porta para mim.**	Please open the door for me.
Faça favor de **não** *escrever* **bobagens.**	Please don't write stupid things.
Façam favor de ajudar **esta senhora.**	Please help this woman.

The same type of request can be made by using *querer* + infinitive or *ter a bondade de* + infinitive.

Quer abrir **a janela para mim?**	Would you mind opening the window for me?
Queres ajudar **o pai a fazer o jantar?**	Would you help your father make dinner?
Tenha a bondade de ler **este formulário para mim.**	Would you be so kind as to read me this form?

14. The Passive Voice

An ordinary sentence is made up of a subject, a verb, an object, and whatever adjectives, adverbs, or other types of words are necessary to give the appropriate information. A sentence with the word order Subject-Verb-Object is said to be in the *active voice*. In the active voice, the subject performs the action of the verb.

If the subject then receives the action of the verb or is acted upon by the object, the sentence is said to be in the *passive voice.* In Portuguese, the passive voice is formed with *ser* and the past participle of the verb, in any tense. The past participle agrees with the subject of the verb in number (singular or plural) and gender (masculine or feminine). The agent is introduced by *por* ("by") and its combinations (see Chapter 28).

> **O cão persegue o gato.**   The dog chases the cat.

This sentence is active; the subject (the dog) is performing the action.

> **O gato é perseguido** *pelo* **cão.**   The cat is chased by the dog.

This sentence is passive; the agent (the dog) is the object of the preposition. The dog is still performing the action, but in a slightly secondary role; the emphasis subtly shifts to the cat, which is being acted upon.

Ser + Past Participle

Active:	**Todas as pessoas admiram o diretor da escola.**	Everyone admires the school principal.
Passive:	**O diretor da escola** *é admirado* **por todas as pessoas.**	The school principal is admired by everyone.
Active:	**O pai da noiva escolheu a lista.**	The bride's father chose the menu.
Passive:	**A lista** *foi escolhida* **pelo pai da noiva.**	The menu was chosen by the bride's father.
Active:	**Nós pedimos costeletas de porco.**	We ordered pork chops.
Passive:	**As costeletas de porco** *foram pedidas* **por nós.**	The pork chops were ordered by us.

Active:	**O rádio vai transmitir uma entrevista com o novo presidente.**	The radio is going to broadcast an interview with the new president.
Passive:	**Uma entrevista com o novo presidente vai** *ser transmitida* **pelo rádio.**	An interview with the new president is going to be broadcast by radio.
Active:	**O Sr. Nóbrega tinha vendido a casa.**	Mr. Nobrega had sold his house.
Passive:	**A casa tinha** *sido vendida* **pelo Sr. Nóbrega.**	The house had been sold by Mr. Nobrega.

The agent can be omitted if it is unknown or indefinite.

O país foi invadido.	The country was invaded.
A senhora tinha sido atacada.	The lady had been attacked.

Estar + Past Participle

Estar may be used with a past participle to describe a state resulting from an action. Again, the past participle agrees in number and gender, just as an adjective would, and can be used with any tense.

A loja *estava fechada.*	The store was closed.
A janela *está partida.*	The window is broken.

Keep in mind that some verbs have two sets of past participles: one to be used with the auxiliary verb *ter,* the other for use with *ser* and *estar* (see Chapter 3).

Reflexive Substitute for the Passive

Often, the reflexive pronoun *se* is used to convey a passive meaning, particularly when the subject of the verb is unknown, undetermined, or irrelevant to understanding the phrase. It is seen on many public signs and notices. *Se* is placed next to the verb according to the rules of positioning (see Chapter 22). The verb is in the active voice in the third person, either singular or plural, depending on the context.

Aqui *fala-se* **português.**	Portuguese is spoken here.
Vende-se **apartamento.**	Apartment for sale.
Não *se ouviram* **as notícias.**	The news was not heard.

Although the sentence *Vende-se apartamento* literally means "Apartment sells itself," its real meaning is "We are selling an apartment." These reflexive sentences can often be rendered in English by using "they," "we," or "people."

Aceitam-se **cartões de crédito.**	We accept credit cards.
	Credit cards are accepted.
Marcou-se **a entrevista para o dia seis.**	They scheduled the interview for the sixth.
	The interview was scheduled for the sixth.

Often the same meaning can be conveyed by simply using the third person plural:

Marcaram **a entrevista para o dia seis.**	They scheduled the interview for the sixth.

Impersonal Use of *Se*

Se can be used with the third person singular to express an indefinite subject ("it," "they," "one," "you").

Como *se diz* **isto em português?**	How do you say this in Portuguese?
Nunca *se sabe* **o que vai acontecer.**	One never knows what's going to happen.
Como *se escreve* **o seu nome?**	How do you write your name?

15. The Personal Infinitive

Portuguese is the only Romance (Latin-based) language that has a personal, or *inflected,* infinitive. As stated earlier, the infinitive is that form of the verb ending in *-ar,* *-er,* and *-ir.* It is equivalent to the English "to + verb."

The General Infinitive

The general infinitive can be used impersonally:

Nadar **faz bem.**
Swimming is good for you.

É difícil *concentrar* **com esta música tão alta.**
It is difficult to concentrate with this music so loud.

It is also used after prepositions:

Antes de *sair,* **vou preparar o jantar.**
Before going out, I'm going to make dinner.

Ela fez os exercícios sem *ter sido pedida* **pelo professor.**
She did the exercises without being asked by the teacher.

The general infinitive can be used as an impersonal command form, often on signs in public places.

Fechar **todas as portas!**
Close all doors!

Finally, it may function as a noun:

O fumar **não é bom para o coração.**
Smoking isn't good for the heart.

The Personal Infinitive

As its name suggests, this type of infinitive is personalized—can be used in its inflected forms (with endings) to refer to whoever is performing the action. It is formed by adding the endings listed below onto the infinitive. The resulting forms may appear to be identical to those of the future subjunctive, but this is only true to a certain extent. Since the future subjunctive is based on the third person plural preterite, any irregularities there are reflected in the future subjunctive form.

falar, to speak		**dizer,** to say	
falar	**falar***mos*	**dizer**	**dizer***mos*
falar*es*	**falar***des*	**dizer***es*	**dizer***des*
falar	**falar***em*	**dizer**	**dizer***em*

Note the contrast with the future subjunctive forms of *dizer (disser, disseres,* etc.).

Usage

In many cases, the personal infinitive can provide a much simpler alternative to complex subjunctive constructions, and is therefore a valuable linguistic tool. Following are its uses.

1. With impersonal expressions

Que bom é *estarmos* **juntos novamente.**	How good it is for us to be together again.
É melhor tu *trancares* **a porta.**	It's better that you lock the door.

The meaning is identical to that of the subjunctive construction:

Que bom que estejamos juntos novamente.
É melhor que tu tranques a porta.

2. After prepositions

Ao *sairem* **da escola, os meninos começaram a gritar.**	When they left the school, the boys began to shout.
Não vou começar até eles *chegarem.*	I'm not going to begin until they arrive.

3. After prepositional phrases

These phrases, among others, may be followed by the personal infinitive: *antes de* ("before"), *depois de* ("after"), *no caso de* ("in case"; "if"), *apesar de* ("in spite of").

No caso deles não *chegarem,* **chamaremos à polícia.**	If they don't arrive, we'll call the police.
Antes de *fazeres* **um erro, verifica o nome do senhor.**	Before you make a mistake, check the man's name.
Apesar de *termos* **telefonado muitas vezes, não havia resposta.**	In spite of our having phoned many times, there was no reply.

Distinguishing Between Verb Subjects

The personal infinitive is often used when a sentence describes two separate actions, especially if there are different subjects for each verb.

Ao *partirem os turistas,* **o dono do hotel ficou aliviado.**

When the tourists left, the hotel owner was relieved.

Antes de *tu chegares,* **o Zé teve um acidente.**

Ze had an accident before you arrived.

However, it can also be used when the subjects are the same:

Depois de *venderem* **a casa,** *os senhores Silva* **emigraram para a Alemanha.**

After selling their house, the Silvas emigrated to Germany.

Ao *chegar o médico,* **viu que a situação era grave.**

When the doctor arrived, he saw that the situation was serious.

Commands

The personal infinitive is also used with *é favor* as a formal imperative, especially in business contexts (written or spoken) and in public announcements.

É favor mandarem **a vossa resposta dentro dum prazo de quinze dias.**

Please send your reply within the next two weeks.

É favor **os concorrentes para o próximo concurso** *chegarem* **ao palco.**

Will the contestants for the next competition please approach the stage?

16. Verbs Followed by a Preposition

The following verbs require a preposition when used before an infinitive. The equivalent English verbs may not always require a preposition, and, when they do, the preposition will not necessarily correspond with the one in Portuguese.

Verbs + *a*

acostumar a	to accustom to
acostumar-se a	to get used to
ajudar a	to help to
aprender a	to learn how to
atrever-se a	to dare to
começar a	to begin to
compelir a	to compel to
decidir-se a	to decide to
desatar a	to burst out
forçar a	to force to
levar a	to cause to
meter-se a	to set out to
obrigar a	to oblige to
ocupar-se a	to busy oneself
pôr-se a	to start to
resignar-se a	to resign oneself to

Verbs + *de*

acabar de	to finish
acusar de	to accuse of
arrepender-se de	to repent from
deixar de	to stop
dissuadir de	to dissuade from
encarregar-se de	to undertake
esquecer-se de	to forget to
fartar-se de	to get tired of
gostar de	to like to
impedir de	to prevent from
isentar de	to exempt from
lembrar-se de	to remember to
parar de	to stop
precisar de	to need to
ter de/que	to have to

Verbs + *em*

concordar em	to agree to
consistir em	to consist of
fazer bem em	to do well to
fazer mal em	to do wrong to
insistir em	to insist on
pensar em	to think of
vacilar em	to hesitate to

Verbs + *por*

acabar por	to end up
começar por	to begin by
esforçar-se por	to make an effort to
lutar por	to fight to
principiar por	to begin by
suspirar por	to long to
terminar por	to end by

Verbs + *com*

contar com	to count on
sonhar com	to dream of

Verbs + *para*

preparar-se para	to prepare to
servir para	to serve to (accomplish a goal)

A **Neusa** *aprendia a* **pintar.**
O **Paulo** *fartou-se de* **ler, e ligou
o rádio.**
Fazes bem em **relaxar; trabalhas
demais.**
Eles vão *esforçar-se por* **chegarem
ao topo da montanha.**
Esta situação *serve para* **ilustrar
as dificuldades de viver num
país estrangeiro.**
Conto com **passar o exame.**
A **briga** *levou-me a* **fazer uma
queixa à polícia.**
As **mulheres foram** *impedidas de*
falarem com os presos.
Estamos a *pensar em* **escrever ao
presidente.**
O **meu pai sempre** *suspirava por*
ganhar a loteria.

Neusa was learning how to paint.
Paul got tired of reading and turned on
the radio.
You do right to relax; you work too
much.
They are going to make an effort to
reach the top of the mountain.
This situation serves to illustrate the
difficulties of living in a foreign
country.
I'm counting on passing the exam.
The fight caused me to make a
complaint to the police.
The women were prevented from
talking to the prisoners.
We're thinking of writing to the
president.
My father always longed to win the
lottery.

Some of these verbs are also used with their preposition when followed by nouns or
pronouns.

Gosto de **bananas.**
Ele *sonhou com* **ela.**
Conto com **a sua presença na
reunião.**
Eles *fartaram-se da* **chuva.**
O **criminoso foi** *acusado do* **roubo.**

Não *me acostumava ao* **calor.**

I like bananas.
He dreamed about her.
I'm counting on your presence at the
meeting.
They got sick of the rain.
The criminal was accused of the
robbery.
I couldn't get used to the heat.

17. Idiomatic Verbs

Idiomatic verbs are those that do not correspond completely with their closest English translation, either in structure or meaning. Following are some of the more common ones. Usually, the verbs have a basic meaning as well as an idiomatic one.

	Basic Definition	Idiomatic Definition
parecer	to seem, to appear	to think
ficar	to remain	to have left over
sobrar	to be more than enough	to have more than enough
faltar	to be missing, to be lacking	to be short of
fazer falta	to be necessary	to need; to miss

Faltam seis pessoas.   Six people are missing.
Falta-me **paciência.**   I'm short of patience.

A tua ajuda faz falta.   Your help is needed.
Faz-lhe falta **a sua namorada.**   He misses his girlfriend.

Elas parecem felizes.   They seem happy.
Parece-me **uma boa idéia.**   I think it's a good idea.

acabar de (+ infinitive), to have just (finished)

Acabo de **comer o almoço.**   I have just eaten lunch.
Eles *acabavam de* **sair.**   They had just gone out.

andar a (+ infinitive), to be (doing something)
andar em, to attend

O Pedro anda a estudar ecologia.   Peter is studying ecology.
Ele anda na Faculdade   He studies in the Science Department.
   de Ciências.

andar bem	to go well; to prosper
andar mal	to go badly
andar de mal a pior	to go from bad to worse
andar de bicicleta	to go by bicycle

doer, to hurt

Doer is used only in the third person. It is singular or plural, depending on the part(s) of the body involved. The English subject becomes the indirect object in Portuguese.

Dói-me **a cabeça.**	My head hurts.
Doem-lhe **os olhos.**	His eyes hurt.

fazer, for, ago, it has been (*time period*) since

Fazer, like *haver,* can be used in expressions of time.

Já *faz* **duas horas que estou a esperar.**	I've been waiting for two hours now.
Fazia **muito tempo que eles não se viam.**	It had been a long time since they'd seen each other.
Fará **um ano que estou aqui.**	It will have been a year since I've been here.

Other Idiomatic Verbal Expressions

estar para	to be at the point of
dar-se bem (com)	to get along well (with)
ir ter com	to go to meet
levar a mal	to take badly
levar (tempo)	to take (time)
pôr casa	to set up house

Eu *estava para* **sair quando telefonou.**	I was about to go out when you phoned.
Ela *foi ter com* **as amigas no centro.**	She went to meet her friends downtown.
Puxa! *Levou-te* **meia hora para ler a carta.**	Wow! It took you half an hour to read the letter.

Part Two: *Essentials of Grammar*

18. Articles

Both the definite and indefinite articles agree with the noun in number and gender.

	Singular	Plural	
Definite Article: "the"	o	os	(*m.*)
	a	as	(*f.*)
Indefinite Article: "a," "an," "some"	um	uns	(*m.*)
	uma	umas	(*f.*)

The masculine plurals of both articles are used to describe mixed groups of males and females, as well as all-male groups.

Singular		Plural	
o carro	the car	os carros	the cars
a mesa	the table	as mesas	the tables
um sapato	a shoe	uns sapatos	some shoes
uma casa	a house	umas casas	some houses

Combinations

Certain prepositions join with articles to form contracted combinations.

por + o = pelo	**Vamos** *pelo* **parque.**	Let's go through the park.
de + o = do	**Não gosto** *do filme.*	I don't like the film.

(For fuller details, see Chapter 28.)

Uses of the Definite Article

Portuguese uses the definite article differently from English in the following situations:

1. With titles, first names, and certain forms of address

O doutor **Pereira é muito simpático.**	Doctor Pereira is very kind.
A Teresa **mora perto de mim.**	Theresa lives near me.
A senhora dona **Ana Maria trabalha no Turismo.**	Ana Maria works in the Tourist Office.

2. With continents, provinces, and countries (excepting Portugal, Angola, Mozambique, Cabo Verde, and several others)

A Europa **é composta por vários países.**	Europe is made up of various countries.
O Algarve **é uma região turística em Portugal.**	The Algarve is a tourist region in Portugal.
Este ano vamos visitar *a França.*	We're going to visit France this year.

3. With names of towns that have an actual meaning

A minha tia mora *no Porto.* (*o porto* = "the port")	My aunt lives in Oporto.
Copacabana fica *no Rio.* (*o rio* = "the river")	Copacabana is in Rio.
Fomos *à Figueira da Foz.* (*a figueira* = "the fig tree"; *a foz* = "mouth of river")	We went to Figueira da Foz.

4. With body parts and clothing, instead of possessive adjectives

Cortei *o dedo.*	I cut my finger.
Deixa-me tirar *o chapéu.*	Let me take off my hat.
Vão lavar *as mãos*!	Go and wash your hands!

5. With nouns used in a general sense

As crianças **gostam de brincar.**	Children like playing.
As frutas **são boas para a saúde.**	Fruit is good for one's health.

6. With names of languages

O português **é a quinta língua mais falada do mundo.**	Portuguese is the fifth most widely spoken language in the world.
A Maria prefere *o francês ao alemão.*	Mary prefers French to German.

However, the definite article with languages is omitted after *de* or *em*, and may not necessarily follow the verbs *aprender, ensinar, entender, estudar, falar,* and *saber.*

O professor *ensina espanhol e italiano.*	The teacher teaches Spanish and Italian.
Ela sabe cantar *em chinês.*	She knows how to sing in Chinese.

7. With units of measure

As laranjas custam quinhentos escudos *o quilo.*	Oranges cost five hundred escudos a kilo.
Comprei o tecido a três dólares *o metro.*	I bought the cloth at three dollars a meter.

8. With meals

Tomo *o almoço* **ao meio-dia.**	I have lunch at noon.
Preparámos *a ceia* **para a tua chegada.**	We prepared supper for your arrival.

9. With certain public institutions

O meu filho adora ir *à escola.*	My son loves going to school.
Vamos para *a cidade.*	Let's go to town.

Omission of Articles

Indefinite Article

The indefinite article is omitted under these circumstances:

1. Before unmodified nouns denoting nationality, rank, and profession

Sou inglesa.	I am an English woman.
O pai do Miguel é capitão.	Michael's father is a captain.
A Maria é gerente duma fábrica.	Mary is the manager of a factory.

2. Before nouns in apposition (with the same function in the sentence), when the noun is not modified.

Cheguei cansada ao meu destino— *Elvas,* **cidade do Alto Alentejo, perto da fronteira espanhola.**	I arrived tired at my destination— Elvas, a city in Alto Alentejo, near the Spanish border.

3. Often when the following words are used:

cem	hundred
mil	thousand
meio	half
semelhante	such
que!	what!
certo	certain
outro	other
tal	such

Pedimos *meia garrafa* **de vinho tinto.**	We ordered half a bottle of red wine.
Certa **pessoa, que é bem conhecida, vai assistir às comemorações na cidade.**	A certain person, who is well known, will attend the celebration in town.
Cem mil **soldados invadiram o país.**	A hundred thousand soldiers invaded the country.

Definite Article

The definite article is omitted:

1. With nouns in apposition, except when the noun is followed by an adjective in the superlative degree

Fomos a *Lisboa, capital* **do país.**	We went to Lisbon, the capital of the country.
Lisboa, a maior cidade **de Portugal, é também a capital.**	Lisbon, the largest city in Portugal, is also the capital.

2. Before a numeral used with the name of a ruler

João I *(primeiro)*	John the First
Afonso V *(quinto)*	Afonso the Fifth

Neuter Article *o*

The neuter article, a remnant of the Latin neuter, is used with masculine singular adjectives to express the abstract, or general, quality of the adjective. In English, the word "thing" often accompanies the adjective.

O importante **é que chegaste são e salvo.**	The important thing is that you arrived safe and sound.
É sempre *o mesmo* **com ele.**	It's always the same thing with him.

O pior **era que tinha perdido a carteira.**	The worst thing was that he had lost his wallet.

Noun Ellipsis

The definite article can be used before *que* or *de* as a demonstrative pronoun.

Os **que foram à Antártica não voltaram.**	Those who went to Antarctica didn't return.
Esta é a cama do Pedro, e esta *a* do Miguel.	This is Peter's bed, and this one is Michael's.

Neuter *o* is used when no direct reference to a noun is given.

Não consigo ouvir *o* que me diz.	I can't hear what you're telling me.

19. Nouns

Gender and Number

Gender

All nouns (things, people, places) in Portuguese are either masculine or feminine words. The gender of words denoting people or animals is determined by the sex.

o homem	man	**a mulher**	woman
o tigre	tiger	**a tigresa**	tigress

Usually, words ending in -*o* are masculine, and those ending in -*a* are feminine.

o casaco	coat	**a porta**	door
o livro	book	**a mesa**	table

Many nouns become feminine by changing the final -*o* to -*a*, or by adding -*a* to the existing masculine form.

o amigo	(male) friend	**a amiga**	(female) friend
o senhor	gentleman	**a senhora**	lady

However, not all nouns fit comfortably into these categories. Many words of Greek origin, for example, end in -*a* but are, in fact, masculine.

o drama	drama	**o telegrama**	telegram

Nouns ending in -*l* and -*r* are generally masculine, while those ending with the letters -*ade*, -*ção*, and -*gem* are generally feminine.

o hotel	hotel
o favor	favor
a cidade	city
a estação	station
a garagem	garage

Since gender is not always obvious from the ending of a word, nouns should be learned together with the appropriate article.

Number

1. The plural of nouns ending in a vowel is formed by simply adding -*s*.

a casa	house	**as casa***s*	houses
a janela	window	**as janela***s*	windows
a árvore	tree	**as árvore***s*	trees

2. The plural of nouns ending in a consonant other than -*l* or -*m* is formed by adding -*es*.

o país	country	**os paí***ses*	countries
o rapaz	boy	**os rapaz***es*	boys

3. Words ending in -*m* form their plural by changing the -*m* to -*ns*.

o jardim	garden	**os jardi***ns*	gardens
o jovem	young person	**os jove***ns*	young people

4. Words ending in -*l* change the -*l* to -*is*. If the word ends in -*il*, -*il* changes to -*is* if the final syllable is stressed, but changes to -*eis* if the syllable is unstressed.

o túnel	tunnel	**os túne***is*	tunnels
o jornal	newspaper	**os jorna***is*	newspapers
o barril	barrel	**os barr***is*	barrels
o réptil	reptile	**os répt***eis*	reptiles

5. Words ending in -*ão* either add a final -*s* or change to -*ões* or -*ães*. The correct plurals for these words can only be learned through memorization.

a mão	hand	**as mão***s*	hands
o portão	gate	**os port***ões*	gates
o cão	dog	**os c***ães*	dogs

6. The masculine plural form is used to denote a combination of two or more masculine and feminine relatives.

o tio	uncle	**os tios**	uncles and aunts
o primo	cousin	**os primos**	cousins
o pai	father	**os pais**	parents

Abstract nouns formed with or followed by an adjective are neuter and have no masculine or feminine gender. They do not change in any way.

o importante	the important (thing)
o difícil	(what's) difficult

20. Adjectives and Adverbs

Adjectives

Agreement

Adjectives are words that describe or give additional information about nouns and pronouns. They agree (have equivalent endings) with the noun in number and gender. If an adjective modifies two or more nouns of different gender, then it is placed in the masculine plural.

o gato preto	the black cat
a porta vermelha	the red door
os senhores satisfeitos	the satisfied gentlemen
as cadeiras antigas	the old chairs
O quadro é bonito.	The picture is pretty.
A casa é cara.	The house is expensive.
Os meninos são altos.	The boys are tall.
As flores são pequenas.	The flowers are small.
O rapaz e a menina são ricos.	The boy and girl are rich.

Gender

Like nouns, adjectives are masculine or feminine, depending on the noun they are describing. In a dictionary or vocabulary list, the adjective is always given in the masculine singular. Adjectives ending in -o switch to a final -a to form the feminine.

o prato redondo	the round plate
a mesa redonda	the round table

If an adjective ends in -e or a *consonant*, the masculine and feminine forms are usually identical, except in adjectives of nationality.

o livro verde	the green book
a saia verde	the green skirt
o tigre feroz	the wild tiger
a raposa feroz	the wild fox

o senhor espanhol	the Spanish man
a senhor*a* espanhol*a*	the Spanish woman

Other masculine-feminine changes include:

	Masculine				Feminine
-or	**sofred*or***	suffering	**+ a**		**sofredor*a***
-ês	**franc*ês***	French	**+ a**		**frances*a***
-u	**n*u***	nude	**+ a**		**nu*a***
-eu	**europ*eu***	European	**> eia**		**europ*éia***
-ão	{ **brincalh*ão***	playful	**> ona**	{	**brincalh*ona***
	{ **crist*ão***	Christian	**> ã**	{	**crist*ã***

There are many exceptions to the rules above.

Number

In general, the plurals of adjectives are formed according to the same rules as for nouns.

o professor simpático	the nice teacher
os menino*s* simpático*s*	the nice boys

a secretária feliz	the happy secretary
as crianç*as* feliz*es*	the happy children

a história incrível	the incredible story
as aventura*s* incríve*is*	the incredible adventures

Position

Adjectives are usually placed *after* the noun they are describing. They can also be found before the noun, but in these cases, certain adjectives change their meaning slightly.

uma senhora *pobre*	a poor woman (in wealth)
uma *pobre* **senhora**	a poor woman (pitiful)

Other adjectives that act in this way include:

	Before Noun	After Noun
grande	great	big
mesmo	same	self
vários	several	various

Ela tem uma *grande* **idéia.**	She has a great idea.
O Pedro *mesmo* **fez o jantar.**	Peter made dinner himself.
Várias **pessoas assistiram ao acidente.**	Several people witnessed the accident.

The following adjectives tend to be used more frequently before the noun, but can be used in either position:

bom	good	**velho**	old
mau	bad	**único**	only
lindo	pretty	**próximo**	next
pequeno	small	**último**	last

Ela é uma *boa* **menina.**	She is a good girl.
Que *lindo* **vestido!**	What a pretty dress!

The cardinal numbers (*primeiro*, "first," *segundo*, "second," etc.) are also normally placed before the noun.

É a *primeira* **rua à direita.**	It's the first street on the right.
A Teresa se casou pela *segunda* **vez.**	Theresa married for the second time.

Suffixes

Instead of using the word *muito* ("very") with an adjective, the suffix *-íssimo* can be added to the adjective instead.

lindo	pretty	**lind**í*ssimo*	very pretty
grande	big	**grand**í*ssimo*	very big, huge

Another widely used suffix, *-inho*, denotes affection or pity.

bonito	pretty	**bonit**inho	cute, really pretty
obrigado	thank you	**obrigad**inho	thanks a lot
coitado	poor, pitiful	**coitad**inho	poor little thing

These endings follow the general rules for plural and feminine forms. For other examples of suffixes, see Chapter 29.

Common Descriptive Adjectives

alto	tall; high	**gordo**	fat
amarelo	yellow	**grande**	big
azul	blue	**laranja**	orange
baixo	short; low	**magro**	thin
bom	good	**mau**	bad
bonito	pretty	**pequeno**	small
branco	white	**pobre**	poor
castanho	brown	**preto**	black
cor-de-rosa	pink	**rápido**	fast
difícil	difficult	**rico**	rich
duro	hard	**simpático**	pleasant, nice
fácil	easy	**triste**	sad
feio	ugly	**verde**	green
feliz	happy	**vermelho**	red

Comparison of Adjectives

To form the comparative of an adjective, place *mais* ("more") or *menos* ("less") before it. To form the superlative, use the definite article with the comparative. Comparative and superlative adjectives must agree with the nouns they modify.

Adjective		Comparative		Superlative	
rico	rich	*mais* **rico**	richer	*o mais* **rico**	the richest
fácil	easy	*mais* **fácil**	easier	*o mais* **fácil**	the easiest
alto	tall	*mais* **alto**	taller	*o mais* **alto**	the tallest

A Maria é rica, mas a Ana é *mais rica.*   Mary is rich, but Anne is richer.

In the superlative, if a noun is expressed, the definite article should go before it.

O Miguel é o mais inteligente.   Michael is the most intelligent.

O Miguel é *o aluno* **mais inteligente.**   Michael is the most intelligent student.

The article may be used with a possessive, which it precedes.

O Miguel é *o meu* **amigo mais inteligente.**   Michael is my most intelligent friend.

De is used to translate "in" after a superlative.

Ele é o professor mais estimado *da* **escola.**	He is the most admired teacher in the school.

Irregular Comparison

Some adjectives have irregular comparatives.

Adjective		Comparative		Superlative	
bom	good	*melhor*	better	o *melhor; óptimo*	the best
mau	bad	*pior*	worse	o *pior; péssimo*	the worst
grande	big	*maior*	bigger	o *maior; máximo*	the biggest
pequeno	small	*menor*	smaller	o *menor; mínimo*	the smallest

Comparison of Age

Students with a knowledge of Spanish will know that the irregular comparatives of *mayor* and *menor* are used in this language to describe relative age. In Portuguese, *mais velho* ("older") and *mais novo* ("younger") are used.

O meu irmão é *mais novo* **que eu.**	My brother is younger than I.
A minha prima *mais velha* **chama-se Verónica.**	My oldest cousin is called Veronica.

Levels of Comparison

Nouns can be compared in a variety of ways. Note that "than" may be expressed as *do que* or *que*.

1. Inequality

do que, que	than
mais _____ **(do) que**	more than
menos _____ **(do) que**	less than

O vestido é *mais caro do que* **a blusa.**	The dress is more expensive than the blouse.
As botas são *menos bonitas que* **as sandálias.**	The boots are not as pretty as the sandals.

Do que (Que) is also used when the clause following the comparison contains a verb.

O senhor *compra* **mais carros do que** *vende.*	The man buys more cars than he sells.

Mais de and *menos de* are used with quantities or numbers.

Tenho *menos de* **quinze dólares.**	I have less than fifteen dollars.
Trabalhou com eles *mais de* **vinte anos.**	He worked with them for more than twenty years.

2. Equality

tão _____ **como, quanto**	as _____ as
tanto _____ **como**	as much _____ as
tantos _____ **como**	as many _____ as

Sou *tão patriótico quanto* **você.**	I'm as patriotic as you.
Ela come *tantos legumes como* **frutas.**	She eats as many vegetables as fruit.

3. Ratio

quanto mais _____ **(tanto) mais**	the more _____ the more
quanto mais _____ **(tanto) menos**	the more _____ the less
quanto menos _____ **(tanto) mais**	the less _____ the more
quanto menos _____ **(tanto) menos**	the less _____ the less

Quanto mais **frutas come,** *tanto mais quer.*	The more fruit he eats, the more he wants.
Quanto maior **seja a mentira,** *menos* **fácil será convencer o professor.**	The bigger the lie, the less easy it will be to convince the teacher.

Adverbs

Adverbs are words that provide information about verbs, adjectives, and other adverbs. Most of them are equivalent to the English adjective + *-ly.*

Formation

Most adverbs are formed by adding *-mente* to the feminine singular adjective form. (If the adjective has only one form for both genders, that form is used.)

rápido	quick	**rápida***mente*	quickly
lento	slow	**lenta***mente*	slowly
fácil	easy	**facil***mente*	easily

If two or more adverbs are used in a series, *-mente* should be placed only at the end of the last one.

A senhora Peixoto trabalha freqüente e *energicamente.*	Mrs. Peixoto works frequently and energetically.

Avoiding the Use of *-mente*

To enhance style and avoid repetition, adverbs ending in *-mente* can be replaced by any of the following:

com + noun
duma maneira + adjective
dum modo + adjective

lindamente	beautifully	**duma maneira linda**	in a lovely manner
bondosamente	kindly	**com bondade**	with kindness
cortesmente	politely	**dum modo cortês**	in a polite way

Adverbs that do not fall into the *-mente* group include:

devagar	slowly		**bem**	well
mal	badly		**cedo**	early

Often, Portuguese uses an adjective when an adverb would be used in English.

A Sara canta *lindo.*	Sarah sings beautifully.
Aprendem muito *rápido.*	They learn very quickly.

Comparison of Adverbs

Comparative adverbs are formed in the same way as comparative adjectives, by using *mais* or *menos*. The superlative also follows the same pattern as for adjectives.

Miguel fala rapidamente.	Michael speaks quickly.
Pedro fala *mais* **rapidamente que Paulo.**	Peter speaks quicker than Paul.
Paulo fala *o mais* **rapidamente de todos.**	Paul speaks the quickest of all.

o mais _____ *possível*	as _____ as possible

o mais **cedo** *possível*	as early as possible
o mais **rapidamente** *possível*	as quickly as possible

Irregular Comparisons

bem	well	**melhor**	better	**o melhor**	the best
mal	badly	**pior**	worse	**o pior**	the worst

Ela escreve *bem,* **mas o irmão escreve** *melhor.*
She writes well, but her brother writes better.

O António canta *pior* **do que o Fábio.**
Anthony sings worse than Fabio.

21. Demonstrative Adjectives and Pronouns

Demonstrative Adjectives

Demonstrative adjectives are used to point out or indicate something or someone. As adjectives, they agree with the noun in number and gender, but unlike other adjectives, demonstratives precede the noun.

Singular		Plural	
este *(m.)*	this	**estes** *(m.)*	these
esta *(f.)*	this	**estas** *(f.)*	these
esse *(m.)*	that	**esses** *(m.)*	those
essa *(f.)*	that	**essas** *(f.)*	those
aquele *(m.)*	that	**aqueles** *(m.)*	those
aquela *(f.)*	that	**aquelas** *(f.)*	those

There are two ways of expressing "that": *esse*, used to refer to objects near to the person being addressed, and *aquele*, for objects at a distance from both parties.

este **relógio**	this clock (or watch)
essa **saia que tu tens**	that skirt you have there
aquele **homem na praça**	that man in the square
estes **dias**	these days
aquelas **casas lá**	those houses over there

Demonstrative Pronouns

Demonstrative pronouns are identical in form to the demonstrative adjectives above. Additionally, there is a singular neuter pronoun, which is used to refer to abstract concepts and indefinable objects. The demonstrative pronouns take the place of nouns, and often are translated as "this one" or "that one."

	Singular		Plural
este *(m.)*	this; this one	**estes** *(m.)*	these
esta *(f.)*	this	**estas** *(f.)*	these
isto *(n.)*	this		
esse *(m.)*	that; that one	**esses** *(m.)*	those
essa *(f.)*	that	**essas** *(f.)*	those
isso *(n.)*	that		
aquele *(m.)*	that; that one	**aqueles** *(m.)*	those
aquela *(f.)*	that	**aquelas** *(f.)*	those
aquilo *(n.)*	that		

Students of Spanish should note that demonstrative pronouns in Portuguese do not carry a written accent.

Este **castelo e** *aquele* **mosteiro lá datam do século quinze.**	This castle and that monastery over there date back to the fifteenth century.
De quem são *estes* **sapatos?**	Whose shoes are these?
Estes **são da Maria.**	These are Mary's.
Que é *isto*?	What is this?
O que é *essa* **coisa estranha que tem na cabeça?**	What's that strange thing you've got on your head?

The appropriate forms of *este* and *aquele* can be used to denote "the former" *(aquele)* and "the latter" *(este)*.

O Rio e Fortaleza são cidades no Brasil; *esta* **fica no norte,** *aquela* **no sul.**	Rio and Fortaleza are cities in Brazil; the latter is in the north, the former in the south.

In this example, *Fortaleza* is the city nearer to the end of the phrase (at the semicolon), and so is referred to as *esta; o Rio* is further from the end of the phrase, and so is referred to as *aquela*.

Comprei uma blusa e uma saia; *esta* **é azul, e** *aquela* **é amarela.**	I bought a blouse and a skirt; the latter is blue, and the former is yellow.

22. Object Pronouns

This book has already introduced the subject pronouns (*eu, tu, ele,* etc.), which are used as the subject of a verb (the person or thing performing the action). Object pronouns receive the action of the verb. They can be direct, indirect, or reflexive and can be used with prepositions.

Direct Object Pronouns

The direct object directly receives the action of the verb.

	Singular		Plural
me	me	**nos**	us
te	you	**vos**	you
o *(m.)*	him; it; you	**os** *(m.)*	them; you
a *(f.)*	her; it; you	**as** *(f.)*	them; you

Vejo-*te.*	I see you.
Ouve-*me*?	Do you hear me?
Compra-*os.*	She buys them.

Changes Following Verbs

With direct object pronouns in the third person (*o, a, os, as*), certain changes occur that aid in pronunciation. These changes take place in the following situations:

1. Following verb forms ending in *-r, -s,* and *-z*

These final letters are omitted, and an *-l* is added to the beginning of the pronoun. In the case of the omission of final *-r*, the following written accents are added to the remaining final vowel of the verb form to maintain stress on the correct syllable:

-ar	**-á**
-er	**-ê**
-ir	**-i** *(no accent)*

Vou ver o meu primo. > **Vou** *vê-lo.*	I'm going to see my cousin. > I'm going to see him.
Compramos a laranja. > *Compramo-la.*	We buy the orange. > We buy it.
A Maria faz o trablaho. > **A Maria** *fá-lo.*	Mary does the work. > Mary does it.

2. Following verb forms ending in *-m, -ão,* and *-õe* (nasal sounds)

The endings are maintained, but an *n* is added before the pronoun to preserve the nasal sound.

Eles compram o bolo. >
 Eles compram-*no.***

They buy the cake. > They buy it.

**As senhoras dão moedas às
 crianças.** > **As senhoras dão-***nas***
 às crianças.**

The women give coins to the
 children. > The women give them
 to the children.

O Pedro põe a mesa. > **O Pedro
 põe-***na.***

Peter sets the table. > Peter sets it.

Indirect Object Pronouns

The indirect object has an indirect relation to the action of the verb. It denotes the person to or for whom the action is performed, as a secondary result of that action's effect on the direct object.

	Singular		Plural
me	to me	**nos**	to us
te	to you	**vos**	to you
lhe	to him, to her, to it, to you	**lhes**	to them, to you

Dá-*me* **o livro.**
Vendo-*lhe* **o carro.**

Give me the book.
I sell the car to her.

To avoid ambiguity with the indirect object pronoun in the third person, the following constructions can be added:

Vendo-lhe o carro *a ele.*
Vendo-lhe a carro *à senhora.*

I sell the car to him.
I sell the car to you.

Reflexive Pronouns

A reflexive pronoun accompanies an appropriate reflexive verb. Reflexive verbs are indicated in the dictionary by *-se*, attached to the infinitive. Some non-reflexive verbs can also be made reflexive. (See Chapter 5. With reflexive verbs, the subject acts upon itself.)

	Singular		Plural
me	myself	**nos**	ourselves
te	yourself	**vos**	yourselves
se	himself, herself, itself, yourself	**se**	themselves, yourselves

Sento-*me* aqui.	I sit down here.
Levantas-*te* cedo?	Do you get up early?
Sirvam-*se*.	Help yourselves.

The -*s* of the first person plural verb form is dropped before the reflexive.

Sentamo-nos **aqui?**	Shall we sit here?

Position of the Object Pronouns

In Portugal, the object pronouns (direct, indirect, or reflexive) are usually attached to the end of the verb by a hyphen. (This is the opposite of the rule in Spanish.) However, in Brazil, object pronouns are more often found preceding the verb in affirmative sentences, especially when a subject pronoun is expressed.

Ele *se* senta perto de mim.	He sits near me.
Ela *se* chama Luisa.	Her name is Louise.

The pronoun precedes the verb, without a hyphen, in the following cases: with conjunctions and adverbs; in "that" clauses (relative clauses); in negative sentences; and with interrogatives and prepositions.

Eu fico aqui enquanto tu *o* compras.	I'll wait here while you buy it.
Sempre *me* sinto mal num barco.	I always feel ill on a boat.
Queria que *lhe* disseste a verdade.	He wanted you to tell him the truth.
Nunca *lhes* dá muita comida.	She never gives them much food.
Quem *se* sentou aqui?	Who sat down here?
Antes de *me* esquecer, preciso de leite.	Before I forget, I need milk.

Position of Pronouns with the Future and Conditional Tenses

When a verb in the future or conditional requires an object pronoun that follows it, the pronoun is inserted in this fashion:

main verb part (infinitive) + pronoun + verb ending.

Eu *falar-lhe-ei* **amanhã.**   I will speak to him tomorrow.

Normal rules of contraction apply:

Fá-lo-iam **se tivessem tempo.**   They would do it if they had the time.

These forms are usually avoided in colloquial language, by omission of the object pronoun or by uses of other tenses.

Eu vou falar com ele amanhã.
Fariam se tivessem tempo.

Contracted Object Pronouns

When a sentence contains two object pronouns, they form a contraction with the indirect pronoun first, followed by the direct. Note that these tend to be used in very formal literary style.

Indirect + Direct				Indirect + Direct			
me	+	**o**	> **mo**	**nos**	+	**o**	> **no-lo**
me	+	**a**	> **ma**	**nos**	+	**a**	> **no-la**
me	+	**os**	> **mos**	**nos**	+	**os**	> **no-los**
me	+	**as**	> **mas**	**nos**	+	**as**	> **no-las**
te	+	**o**	> **to**	**vos**	+	**o**	> **vo-lo**
te	+	**a**	> **ta**	**vos**	+	**a**	> **vo-la**
te	+	**os**	> **tos**	**vos**	+	**os**	> **vo-los**
te	+	**as**	> **tas**	**vos**	+	**as**	> **vo-las**
lhe	+	**o**	> **lho**	**lhes**	+	**o**	> **lho**
lhe	+	**a**	> **lha**	**lhes**	+	**a**	> **lha**
lhe	+	**os**	> **lhos**	**lhes**	+	**os**	> **lhos**
lhe	+	**as**	> **lhas**	**lhes**	+	**as**	> **lhas**

Ele deu-no-lo**.**   He gave it to us.
Ela não no-lo **deu.**   She did not give it to us.
Disseram-mo**.**   They told me.
Deram-lhas**.**   They gave them to them.

Confusion may arise from the ambiguity found in this last example. To avoid this, use the prepositional forms *a ele, a ela, aos senhores,* etc.

Deram-lhas *aos senhores.*   They gave them to you.
Deram-lhas *a eles.*   They gave them to them.

Avoidance of Contracted Forms

These awkward constructions are often spontaneously omitted from Portuguese, as too are the more simple object forms.

Emprestas-me os copos?	Will you lend me the glasses?
Sim, *empresto.*	Yes, I will (lend them to you).
A Ana gosta da sopa?	Does Anne like the soup?
Sim, *gosta.*	Yes, she does (like it).

Object Pronouns with Prepositions

When object pronouns follow a preposition, they take another form.

Singular		Plural	
mim	me	**nós**	us
ti	you	**vós**	you
ele	him	**eles**	them
ela	her	**elas**	them
si	himself, herself, itself, yourself	**si**	themselves, yourselves
você	you, yourself	**vocês**	you, yourselves

Ela pensa sempre *em mim.*	She always thinks about me.
Não existem mentiras *entre nós.*	There are no lies between us.
Ele gosta de fazer coisas *para elas.*	He likes to do things for them.
Elas gostam de fazer coisas *para si.*	They like to do things for themselves.

To add clarity to a sentence, the appropriate forms of *mesmo* or *próprio* may be added.

Ela faz para si *mesma.*	She does it for herself.
Comprámos o bolo para nós *próprios.*	We bought the cake for ourselves.

Object Pronouns with the Preposition *com*

The object pronouns combine with the preposition *com* in the following ways:

	Singular		Plural
comigo	with me	**conosco**	with us
contigo	with you	**convosco**	with you
com ele	with him	**com eles**	with them
com ela	with her	**com elas**	with them
com você	with you	**com vocês**	with you
consigo	with him(self), her(self), your(self)	**consigo**	with them(selves), your(selves)

Vens *comigo*?	Are you coming with me?
O João foi *com eles* **ao museu.**	John went with them to the museum.
Tem o seu passaporte *consigo*?	Have you got your passport with you?

For a comprehensive view of prepositions, see Chapter 27.

23. Relative Pronouns

Relative pronouns are used to join (relate) a dependent clause to the main clause of a sentence. A dependent clause refers to something or someone previously mentioned (the antecedent). The relative pronoun can be a subject, an object, or the object of a preposition. The relative pronouns most commonly used are:

que	who, whom, which, that
quem	who, whom
o qual	who, whom, which, that
o que	which

Pronouns as Relatives

1. *Que* refers to both people and things and can be either a subject or an object. Following a preposition, it refers only to things.

O professor *que* **ensina inglês é muito velho.**	The teacher who teaches English is very old.
O professor *que* **vimos hoje é alemão.**	The teacher whom we saw today is German.
Temos uma mesa *que* **queremos pintar.**	We have a table that we want to paint.
A caixa em *que* **guardo os jornais é de madeira.**	The box in which I keep the newspapers is wooden.

2. *Quem* is used only to refer to people and follows a preposition.

A senhora *com quem* **fala é a minha tia.**	The lady with whom you are talking is my aunt.
O rapaz *para quem* **comprei a rosa mora aqui.**	The boy for whom I bought the rose lives here.

Quem can also be used without a specific antecedent.

Quem **estuda muito, aprende muito.**	He who studies a lot, learns a lot.
Procuro *quem* **possa pintar a casa.**	I'm looking for someone who can paint the house.
Não há *quem* **ensine latim nesta escola.**	There's no one who teaches Latin in this school.

3. *O qual* can be used in place of *que*, when referring to people, to avoid ambiguity. The definite article agrees in gender and number with the antecedent. Note the following ambiguous sentence:

Vamos falar com a prima do Miguel *que* **já conhecemos do baile.**	Let's go and talk to Michael's cousin, whom we already know from the dance.

It is unclear in the above example whether the speaker had met Michael or his cousin at the dance. The use of the feminine *a qual* in the following sentence leaves no doubt that this reference was to the cousin.

Vamos falar com a prima do Miguel, *a qual* **já conhecemos do baile.**

O qual is also used with prepositions, especially compound prepositions (consisting of more than one word).

Este é o castelo detrás *do qual* **há um belo jardim.**	This is the castle, behind which is a lovely garden.
Visitámos a cidade *na qual* **nasci.**	We visited the city in which I was born.

4. *O que* is a neuter relative, used when there is no specific noun as an antecedent. It refers to the preceding phrase as a whole.

Ela comprou o carro, *o que* **zangou o seu marido.**	She bought the car, which angered her husband.
Disseram-me pouco, *o que* **me preocupou.**	They told me little, which worried me.

Quanto (-s, -a, -as) "all . . . that" is often used in the place of *tudo o que* ("all of which").

Deram-me *quantos* **selos tinham.**	They gave me all the stamps that they had.

5. Although *cujo (-s, -a, -as)* ["whose," "of whom," "of which"] is a relative adjective and as such agrees in gender and number with the noun it modifies, it is used in the same way as relative pronouns.

Este é o meu amigo *cujos* **pais são diplomatas.**	This is my friend whose parents are diplomats.
Visitámos o museu, *cujas* **portas são amarelas.**	We visited the museum, the doors of which are yellow.

24. Possessive Pronouns and Adjectives

Both the possessive pronouns and their corresponding adjectives are identical in form, and both agree in number and gender with the thing possessed, not the possessor. They are both preceded by the definite article, although it tends to be dropped for the pronoun. Brazilian Portuguese often omits the article with both pronoun and adjective.

Possessive Adjectives

	Singular		Plural	
	Masculine	Feminine	Masculine	Feminine
my	o meu	a minha	os meus	as minhas
your	o teu	a tua	os teus	as tuas
his, her, your	o seu	a sua	os seus	as suas
our	o nosso	a nossa	os nossos	as nossas
your	o vosso	a vossa	os vossos	as vossas
their, your	o seu	a sua	os seus	as suas

o meu **casaco**	my coat
a tua **irmã**	your sister
os seus **sapatos**	his (her, your, their) shoes
as nossas **casas**	our houses
o vosso **livro**	your book
a sua **vida**	her (his, your, their) life

O(s) seu(s) and a(s) sua(s) can be ambiguous, since they have a variety of meanings. In order to avoid confusion, the following forms can be used after the noun:

dele	of him
dela	of her
deles	of them (m.)
delas	of them (f.)

as cadeiras dele	his chairs
o gato delas	their cat
as flores dela	her flowers

In Portuguese, possessive adjectives are used less than in English—especially with parts of the body, clothing that belongs to the subject of the verb, and when the possession is obvious. Instead, the definite article is used on its own.

Os meninos lavam *as* **mãos.**	The children wash their hands.
A Maria põe *as* **botas.**	Mary puts her boots on.
O Miguel tira *o* **chapéu.**	Michael takes his hat off.
Eu não tinha nada *no* **bolso.**	I had nothing in my pocket.

Possessive Pronouns

The forms for possessive adjectives and pronouns are identical. The definite article tends to be omitted after forms of the verb *ser*. Again, they agree with the thing possessed. These pronouns take the place of nouns and are equivalent to the English "mine," "yours," "his," "hers," "its," "ours," and "theirs."

A *minha* **é azul.**	Mine is blue.
O *seu* **era bom.**	Yours (his, hers, theirs) was good.
Os *nossos* **são pequenos.**	Ours are small.
Esta mesa não é *tua.*	This table isn't yours.
De quem é este copo? É *meu.*	Whose glass is this? It's mine.

To avoid ambiguity in the third person forms, the following forms can be used:

o, a, os, as dele	his
o, a, os, as dela	hers
o, a, os, as deles	theirs *(m.)*
o, a, os, as delas	theirs *(f.)*

A nossa casa é enorme, mas *a deles* **é pequena.**	Our house is huge, but theirs is small.
O amigo do Paulo era pobre; *o dela* **era rico.**	Paul's friend was poor; hers was rich.
Os meus pais são simpáticos; *os deles* **não.**	My parents are nice; theirs are not.

25. Negatives, Interrogatives, and Exclamations

Negatives

Não ("no," "not") always precedes the verb, but it can follow other words. Portuguese uses double negatives in the following sequence:

não + verb + another negative.

Common Negatives

não   no, not

O carro *não* **parou.**	The car did not stop.
Agora *não.*	Not now.

nada   nothing, anything

Não **há** *nada* **para beber.**	There is nothing to drink.
Ele *não* **quer** *nada.*	He doesn't want anything.
Nada **aconteceu.**	Nothing happened.

ninguém   nobody, anybody

Não **falou** *ninguém.*	Nobody spoke.
Não **havia** *ninguém* **para nos receber.**	There wasn't anybody to welcome us.
Ninguém **saiu.**	Nobody went out.

nenhum   no, none, any

Não **existe** *nenhum* **problema.**	There is no problem.
Não **falei com** *nenhuma* **delas.**	I didn't speak to any of them.
Nenhum **sapato me servia.**	No shoe fit me.

também não   not either, neither

Ela *não* **foi ao cinema; o irmão** *também não.*	She didn't go to the movies; neither did her brother.

nem   nor, neither

Ele *não* **gosta de café,** *nem* **de chá.**	He does not like coffee or tea.
A Teresa *não* **fala muito.** *Nem* **eu!**	Theresa does not talk much. Neither do I!

nem _____ nem   neither _____ nor, any _____ or

Não **tenho** *nem* **carne** *nem* **peixe.**	I haven't got any meat or fish.
O Sr. Silva *não* **gosta** *nem* **de ler,** *nem* **de ver televisão.**	Mr. Silva doesn't like reading or watching television.

nem sequer   not even

Nem sequer **escreve à sua filha.**	He doesn't even write to his daughter.

nunca, jamais   never, ever

Eles *nunca* **limpam o quarto.**	They never clean their room.
Não **te vejo** *nunca*.	I never see you.
Jamais **te esquecerei.**	I'll never forget you.

Negative Responses

In responding to a question in a negative way, Portuguese tends to use a double negative.

Gostas de leite?	Do you like milk?
Não, não **gosto.**	No, I don't.

Quer escutar música?	Do you want to listen to music?
Não **quero,** *não*.	No, I don't.

Interrogatives

To make a question out of a general statement, simply raise the intonation of your voice at the end of the sentence.

Estás a falar com ela.	You are talking to her.
Estás a falar com ela?	Are you talking to her?

Interrogatives are classified as adjectives, pronouns, or adverbs.

Interrogative Adjectives and Pronouns

que?, o que?	what?
quem?	who?
a quem?	to whom?
qual?, quais?	what?, which one/s?
quanto?, -a?	how much?
quantos?, -as?	how many?

O que **vão comprar?**	What are you going to buy?
Qual **é a sua escola?**	Which one is your school?
Quanto **custa a bicicleta?**	How much does the bicycle cost?
Quantas **laranjas tem?**	How many oranges do you have?
Quem **falou?**	Who spoke?

Interrogative Adverbs

como?	how?
quando?	when?
onde?	where?
porque?	why?

Como **se escreve o seu nome?**	How do you write your name?
Quando **partiram?**	When did they leave?
Onde **fica o banco?**	Where is the bank?
Porque **não estuda mais?**	Why don't you study more?

Interrogatives with Prepositions

Some of these interrogatives may also be used with certain prepositions. Here are some of the more common ones:

para quem?	for whom?
com quem?	with whom?
de quem?	of whom?, whose?
aonde?	where to?
para onde?	where to?
de onde?, donde?	from where?
em que?	in which?

Para quem **compra o presente?**	Who are you buying the present for?
Aonde **vai a estas horas?**	Where are you going at this hour?
Em que **loja achou o livro?**	In which store did you find the book?

Portuguese questions often use *é que* in an extended interrogative form (like the French *est-ce que*) to add emphasis.

Onde é que **nós vamos?**	Where is it that we're going?
Porque é que **a viagem sempre demora?**	Why is it that the trip always takes a long time?

Exclamations

que!	what!, what a!, how!
quanto, -a!	how much!
quantos, -as!	how many!
qual!	what!, indeed!

Que **sorte!**	What luck!
Que **quadro bonito!**	What a beautiful picture!
Quantas **flores!**	What a lot of flowers!
Qual **bestseller!**	Bestseller indeed!

26. *Todo* and *Tudo*; *Ambos* and *Cada*

Todo

Todo ("all," "every," "the whole") agrees in number and gender with any correspond-ing noun.

Toda **a loja estava arrumada.**	The whole store was tidied up.
Todos **os alunos foram ao castelo.**	All the students went to the castle.
Toda **pessoa que entra será revistada.**	Every person who enters will be searched.

Translated as "all" or "the whole," *todo* can be placed either before or after the noun.

$$\left.\begin{array}{l} todo \textbf{ o inverno} \\ \textbf{o inverno } todo \end{array}\right\}$$ all winter, the whole winter

The definite article can be omitted when the word accompanying *todo* does not nor-mally call for an article.

Fomos nós *todos.*	All of us went.
Todas **aquelas mulheres são médicas.**	All those women are doctors.

Adverbial Use

Todo can be used in the singular as an adverb.

Tens a perna *toda* **torcida.**	Your leg is all twisted.
O carro está *todo* **sujo.**	The car's all dirty.

Tudo

Tudo ("all," "everything") is a neuter pronoun, and as such it never changes form.

Ela compra *tudo* **que vê.**	She buys everything she sees.
Tudo **isto é muito mau.**	All of this is very bad.
Primeiro que *tudo*, **não se esqueça de sorrir.**	Above all, don't forget to smile.

Ambos

Ambos ("both"), like *todo,* is used with a definite article when describing a noun, and without when used alone or with pronouns or demonstratives.

Ambos **os irmãos são bombeiros.**	Both brothers are firefighters.
Ambas **as casas são antigas.**	Both houses are old.
Ambos **partiram.**	They both departed.
Nós *ambos* **fomos à festa.**	We both went to the party.

Cada

Cada ("each," "every") does not vary in form. It is used without a definite article and serves for both singular and plural nouns.

Cada **semana vou à cidade.**	Every week I go to town.
Íamos à praia *cada* **fim de semana.**	We used to go to the beach every weekend.
Ela toma o remédio *cada* **três horas.**	She takes her medicine every three hours.
Cada **um de nós vai receber uma carta.**	Each one of us is going to receive a letter.
Cada **uma é bonita.**	Each one is pretty.

27. Prepositions

Prepositions are words generally indicating place, time, and manner. As such, they serve to clarify the relationship between other words (nouns, pronouns, verbs, and adverbs). They can be simple, like *em* ("in," "on") or more complex, like *dentro de* ("inside").

Simple Prepositions

a	at, to	**em**	in, on, at
ante	before	**entre**	between, among
após	after	**para**	for, to, toward
até	up to, until	**por**	for, by, through
com	with	**sem**	without
contra	against	**sob**	below, under
de	of, from, about	**sobre**	on, on top of, about
desde	since, from		

Ele foi *ao* **museu.**	He went to the museum.
O chá *com* **limão faz bem** *para* **a tosse.**	Tea with lemon is good for a cough.
O livro está *na* **estante.**	The book is on the shelf.
O Pedro não quer ir *sem* **o seu amigo.**	Peter does not want to go without his friend.

For a fuller explanation of *para* and *por* and their differences, see Chapter 28.

Compound Prepositions

à frente de	at the front of	**detrás de**	behind
além de	beyond, besides	**em cima de**	on top of
antes de	before	**em frente de**	in front of
ao redor de	around	**em volta de**	around, about
através de	through, across	**fora de**	outside
à volta de	around, about	**longe de**	far (from)
debaixo de	under	**perto de**	near, near by
defronte de	opposite	**por cima de**	over, above
dentro de	inside	**por dentro de**	(from) inside
depois de	after	**por volta de**	around, about

À frente da **casa há um belo jardim.**	At the front of the house is a lovely garden.
Vamos cortar *através da* **praça.**	Let's cut across the square.
As jóias estão guardadas *dentro dum* **cofre.**	The jewelery is kept inside a safe.
Eles moram *perto da* **escola.**	They live near the school.

Verbs with Prepositions

In addition to those verbs discussed in Chapter 16 that take on specific meanings when followed by a preposition, verbs in the infinitive may also be preceded by prepositions.

Olharam-se *sem* **dizer nada.**	They looked at each other without saying anything.
Além de **comprar o jantar, também pagou o táxi.**	Besides buying the dinner, he also paid for the taxi.
Depois de **acordar, levanto-me devagar.**	After waking up, I get up slowly.

A preposition + *que* + verb is a form known as a *compound conjunction.* These conjunctions often call for a subjunctive verb form and may require some practice.

Comprei o livro *para que* **tu** *possas* **ler mais.**	I bought the book so that you can read more.

Time Prepositions

1. **a,** at

A **que horas abre o banco?**	(At) what time does the bank open?
Abre *às* **oito e meia.**	It opens at eight thirty.
Todos gritaram *ao* **mesmo tempo.**	They all shouted at the same time.

2. **antes de,** before

Ela chegou *antes de* **mim.**	She arrived before me.
Temos de partir *antes das* **sete.**	We have to leave before seven.

3. à volta de
   por volta de
   por   } about, around
   lá para *(used in Brazil)*

    A festa começa *pelas* **dez horas.**   The party begins around ten.
    Chegou *lá para* **meia-noite.**   She arrived at about midnight.

4. depois de, após, after

    A loja abre só *depois do* **meio-dia.**   The store only opens after noon.
    O calor continuou, semana *após*   The heat continued, week after week.
    semana.

5. de _____ a, desde _____ até, from _____ to, from _____ until

    O correio abre *das* **8.30** *às* **17.30.**   The post office is open from 8:30 A.M.
        to 5:30 P.M.

    Ficámos à espera *desde* **as quatro**   We waited from four until nine at night.
    até **as nove da noite.**

Contractions

The following prepositions combine and contract with definite and indefinite articles and demonstratives.

Preposition	Def. Article	Indef. Article	Demonstrative
a	ao, à, aos, às		
em	no, na, nos, nas	num, numa, nuns, numas	neste, nesta, nestes, nestas, nisto
			nesse, nessa, nesses, nessas, nisso
			naquele, naquela, naqueles, naquelas, naquilo
de	do, da, dos, das	dum, duma, duns, dumas	deste, desta, destes, destas
			desse, dessa, desses, dessas, disso
			daquele, daquela, daqueles, daquelas, daquilo
por	pelo, pela, pelos, pelas		

Foram *ao* **museu.**	They went to the museum.
Moro *num* **apartamento.**	I live in an apartment.
Gosto mais *daquele* **casaco.**	I like that coat the best.
Vamos correr *pelas* **ruas.**	Let's run through the streets.

Other contractions, such as *de* + *algum* > *dalgum,* can appear in the written language as two separate words. Even then, they are sometimes pronounced as one when spoken.

28. *Por* and *Para*

The prepositions *por* and *para* can cause some confusion, since their varied meanings sometimes overlap. *Por* contracts with the definite article to form *pelo (-a, -os, -as)*.

Por

Por ("for," "through," "by," "along," "per," "because of") is used in the following situations:

1. Place through, by, or along which

Vamos passar *pelo* **parque.**	Let's go through the park.
Gostamos de andar *pela* **beira-mar.**	We like walking beside the seashore.

2. Expressions of time: through, during, for

Dançámos *pela* **noite inteira.**	We danced throughout the whole night.
Fomos ao Canadá *por* **dez dias.**	We went to Canada for ten days.
Esperei *por* **um momento.**	I waited for a moment.

3. Exchange, price for, substitution for

Ela pagou trinta dólares *por* **aquela blusa.**	She paid thirty dollars for that blouse.
Estou doente; fazes a aula *por* **mim?**	I'm ill; will you take the class for me?

4. By or per unit of measure

Como se vendem as laranjas? *Por* **quilo.**	How are the oranges sold? By the kilo.
O salário mínimo é de quatrocentos dólares *por* **mês.**	The minimum wage is four hundred dollars a month.

5. Way or means by

Entraram na casa *por* **força.**	They entered the house by force.
Foi só *por* **acaso que te encontrei.**	It was merely by chance that I found you.

6. Because of, on account of, for

A "Miss" foi eleita não só *pela*
   beleza, mas também *pela*
   inteligência.

The beauty queen was chosen not
   only for her beauty, but also for her
   intelligence.

A região do Douro é conhecida
   pelos bons vinhos.

The Douro region is well known for
   its good wines.

7. To go for, to send for

Se for à cidade, vai ao talho
   por um frango.

If you're going to town, go to the
   butcher shop for a chicken.

Mandou-me ao correio *por* dez
   selos.

She sent me to the post office for
   ten stamps.

8. On behalf of, for the sake of, for

Este ano não votei *por* partido
   nenhum.

This year I didn't vote for any party.

Fez tudo *por* ela.

He did everything for her.

9. Motive or reason for

Levou o dinheiro *por* necessidade.
Morreram todos *pela* crença.

He took the money by necessity.
They all died for their beliefs.

10. On the occasion of

Receberam muitos presentes *pelo*
   seu aniversário de casamento.

They received a lot of presents for
   their wedding anniversary.

No Brasil, é comum festejar na
   praia *pelo* Reveillon.

In Brazil it's common to celebrate
   on the beach on New Year's Eve.

11. After a passive verb, to indicate agent

A janela foi partida *por* uma pedra.
Estes exercícios não foram feitos
   por você.

The window was broken by a stone.
These exercises were not done by you.

Para

Para ("for," "to," "in order to," "toward") is used in the following situations:

1. Use: for

Esta é uma caixa *para* **guardar dinheiro.**	This is a box for keeping money in.
A nova loja vende tudo *para* **artesanato.**	The new shop sells everything for arts and crafts.

2. Destination (place or person): towards, for

Fomos primeiro *para* **a Grécia.**	We went to Greece first.
A Maria foi *para* **casa.**	Mary went home.
Este bolo não é *para* **ti.**	This cake is not for you.

3. Purpose: in order to

Comprei este tecido *para* **fazer umas calças.**	I bought this cloth to make some pants.
Ela pinta quadros *para* **vender.**	She paints pictures to sell.

4. Time expressions: for, by, towards

Pode fazê-lo *para* **amanhã?**	Can you do it by tomorrow?
As férias começam lá *para* **o fim de julho.**	The vacation begins toward the end of July.

29. Suffixes

Suffixes are small additions to the ends of words that give those words additional meaning. They can indicate larger or smaller size, change adjectives and verbs into nouns, and transform one noun into several others. The most common suffixes are *-mente* (for adverbs), *-inho, -zinho, -zito, -ão, -zarrão, -ona, -zada,* and *-zeiro.*

General Formation

If a word ends in a consonant, the suffix is added to the full word form, unless the word ends in *-m, -ão,* or *-l* and is used with a suffix beginning with *z*. In this case, *-m* becomes *-n*. Plural forms drop the final *-s* before the suffix. All words originally carrying a written accent lose it.

o jovem	young person	**+ zinho**	=	**o joven***zinho*	kid
os jovens	young people			**os joven***zinhos*	kids
o pão	loaf of bread	**+ zinho**	=	**o pão***zinho*	bread roll
os pães	loaves of bread			**os pãe***zinhos*	bread rolls

Diminutives

Diminutives *(-inho, -zinho, -zito)* are used to describe a person or object as small or cute and can denote affection.

Words ending in unstressed *-o* or *-a* lose that ending and add *-inho* or *-inha.* Other words usually add *-zinho* or *-zinha.*

a mesa	table	**a mes***inha*	little table
doente	ill	**doent***inho*	slightly sick
a manhã	morning	**a manhã***zinha*	early morning
pobre	poor	**pobre***zinho*	poor little thing
a coitada	poor woman	**a coitad***inha*	poor little woman
a casa	house	**a cas***inha*	small house
um livro	book	**um livr***inho*	booklet
a mãe	mother	**a mãe***zinha*	dear mother
Pedro	Peter	**Pedr***inho*	Pete
o hotel	hotel	**o hotel***zinho*	small hotel
um pouco	a little	**um pouqu***inho*	a little bit
a filha	daughter	**a filh***inha*	young, dear daughter

Augmentatives

Augmentatives *(-ão, -zarrão, -ona)* are suffixes used to describe a person or object as large, strong, or ugly and can be perjorative. In the case of *-ão*, it is added onto words ending in a consonant and replaces the final letter of most words ending in vowels. Feminine nouns become masculine in the *-ão* augmentative. The augmentative *-zarrão* follows the rules for suffixes beginning with *-z*, while *-ona* is only used for words describing girls and women.

a **carta**	letter	o **cart**ão	card; cardboard
a **casa**	house	o **casar**ão	mansion
a **garrafa**	bottle	o **garraf**ão	jug
a **mulher**	woman	a **mulher**ona	big woman
a **faca**	knife	o **facalh**ão	big knife
a **solteira**	single woman	a **solteir**ona	spinster
a **porta**	door	o **port**ão	gate
a **sala**	room	o **sal**ão	large room
o **gato**	cat	o **gat**ão	big cat
o **cão**	dog	o **can**zarrão	big dog

Both diminutive and augmentative forms can be awkward to use correctly and require practice at first. Diminutive forms are extremely common in Portugal and Brazil.

Other Common Suffixes

-ada, -ado (-ful, group of)

a **colher**	spoon	a **colher**ada	spoonful
a **criança**	child	a **crianç**ada	group of children
o **punho**	fist	o **punh**ado	handful
o **ninho**	nest	a **ninh**ada	brood
o **rapaz**	boy	a **rapaz**iada	gang of boys

-ria, -aria (place where an article is made or sold)

a **fruta**	fruit	a **frut**aria	fruitstand
o **pastel**	pastry	a **pastel**aria	bakery *(selling cake)*
o **pão**	bread	a **pad**aria	bakery *(selling bread)*
o **livro**	book	a **livr**aria	bookstore
o **sapato**	shoe	a **sapat**aria	shoestore; shoe repair shop
o **peixe**	fish	a **peix**aria	fishstore

-eira (the tree a fruit has come from)

a maçã	apple	**a maci***eira*	apple tree
a laranja	orange	**a laranj***eira*	orange tree
a amêndoa	almond	**a amendo***eira*	almond tree
a banana	banana	**a banan***eira*	banana plant
o figo	fig	**a figu***eira*	fig tree
a cereja	cherry	**a cerej***eira*	cherry tree

-eza, -ura, -ade (adjectives changed into nouns, usually abstract)

grande	large	**grand***eza*	greatness
alto	tall	**alt***ura*	height
sincero	sincere	**sincerid***ade*	sincerity
triste	sad	**trist***eza*	sadness
gordo	fat	**gord***ura*	fat, fatness
mau	bad	**mald***ade*	badness, evil

-dor, -dora (a verb changed into the person performing the action when added to the infinitive of a verb, after dropping the final *-r*)

educar	to educate	**educa***dor*	educator
navegar	to navigate	**navega***dor*	sailor; navigator
trabalhar	to work	**trabalha***dor*	worker
nadar	to swim	**nada***dor*	swimmer
pescar	to fish	**pesca***dor*	fisherman
observar	to observe	**observa***dor*	observer

30. Time

Days of the Week

segunda-feira	Monday
terça-feira	Tuesday
quarta-feira	Wednesday
quinta-feira	Thursday
sexta-feira	Friday
sábado	Saturday
domingo	Sunday

Weekdays are feminine, and it is common in the spoken language to drop the *-feira* suffix from each one. The days of the weekend are masculine. The prepositions *em* and *a* are used with days of the week.

na quarta-feira	on Wednesday
nas quartas	on Wednesdays
A camioneta para Lisboa parte *às segundas* **e** *às quintas*.	The bus to Lisbon departs on Mondays and Thursdays.
Hoje é *sábado*.	Today is Saturday.
Vamos visitar Chicago *na sexta*.	We're going to visit Chicago on Friday.
Todos *os domingos* **eles vão à missa.**	They go to Mass every Sunday.

Months of the Year

janeiro	January	**julho**	July
fevereiro	February	**agosto**	August
março	March	**setembro**	September
abril	April	**outubro**	October
maio	May	**novembro**	November
junho	June	**dezembro**	December

Seasons of the Year

a primavera	spring
o verão	summer
o outono	fall
o inverno	winter

Dates

Cardinal numbers (one, two, three, etc.) are used with dates, including (in Portugal) the first—*o dia um*. In Brazil, the first of the month is referred to as *o dia primeiro* or simply, *o primeiro*.

Que dia é hoje?
Quantos são hoje? } What is the date today?
A quantos estamos?

É o dia vinte e três.	It's the twenty-third.
Hoje são onze.	It's the eleventh today.
Estamos a vinte e dois.	It's the twenty-second.
É o quinze de setembro.	It's the fifteenth of September.
Nasceu ao seis de julho de 1971.	He was born on July 6, 1971.

Divisions of Time

o segundo	second		**o dia**	day
o minuto	minute		**meio-dia**	noon
a hora	hour		**a semana**	week
meia hora	half an hour		**quinze dias**	two weeks
um quarto de hora	quarter of an hour		**o mês**	month
a manhã	morning		**o ano**	year
a tarde	afternoon		**a estação**	season
a noite	night		**o século**	century
meia-noite	midnight			

Expressions of Time

agora	now	ontem	yesterday
agora mesmo	right now	anteontem	the day before yesterday
já	right now		
hoje	today	a semana passada	last week
esta noite	tonight	a semana que vem	next week
ontem à noite	last night	a semana próxima	next week
anteontem à noite	the night before last	o mês passado	last month
		a quinta passada	last Thursday
amanhã	tomorrow	o domingo que vem	next Sunday
depois de amanhã	the day after tomorrow	todo o dia	all day
		ao anoitecer	at nightfall
de madrugada	early in the morning	todos os dias	every day
		cada dia	every day
de manhã	in the morning	todo o tempo	all the time
de tarde	in the afternoon	ontem à tarde	yesterday afternoon
à noite	at night		
amanhã de manhã	tomorrow morning		
ao amanhecer	at daybreak		

Indefinite Time

no princípio do mês	at the beginning of the month
no meio da semana	in the middle of the week
ao fim (aos fins) do ano	at the end of the year

Time of Day

Que horas são?	What time is it?
Tem as horas?	Do you have the time?
A que horas sai?	What time is she leaving?
É a uma.	It's one o'clock.
É meio-dia.	It's noon.
É meia-noite.	It's midnight.
São duas da tarde.	It's two p.m.
Você chega à uma.	You arrive at one o'clock.
Chego às nove da noite.	I arrive at nine P.M.

Time *after* the hour is expressed by adding the number of minutes, up to thirty, to the hour.

São quatro *e dez.*	It's ten after four.
É uma *e um quarto.*	It's a quarter after one.

Time up to thirty minutes *before* the hour is expressed in three ways:

1. By subtracting the minutes from the nearest next full hour
2. By using the number of minutes to the hour + *para*
3. With *faltar* + the number of minutes to the hour + *para.*

Às dez *menos vinte.*	At twenty to ten.
São *cinco para* **as três.**	It's five to three.
Faltam dez para **meia-noite.**	It's ten minutes before midnight.
É *um quarto para* **a uma.**	It's a quarter to one.

The twenty-four hour clock, commonly used in timetables, is more straightforward.

O comboio (*Br.* **trem) parte às** *vinte e duas e cinqüenta.*	The train leaves at 22:50.
O barco chega às *quinze e vinte e nove.*	The boat arrives at 15:29.

The Cardinal Points

o norte	north		**o nordeste**	northeast
o sul	south		**o sudeste**	southeast
o leste	east		**o noroeste**	northwest
o oeste	west		**o sudoeste**	southwest

31. Numerals

Cardinal Numbers

0	zero	30	trinta
1	um, uma	31	trinta e um, uma
2	dois, duas	32	trinta e dois, duas
3	três	40	quarenta
4	quatro	50	cinqüenta
5	cinco	60	sessenta
6	seis	70	setenta
7	sete	80	oitenta
8	oito	90	noventa
9	nove	100	cem, cento*
10	dez	101	cento e um, uma
11	onze	110	cento e dez
12	doze	200	duzentos, (-as)
13	treze	300	trezentos, (-as)
14	catorze	400	quatrocentos, (-as)
15	quinze	500	quinhentos, (-as)
16	dezasseis (*Br.* dezesseis)	600	seiscentos, (-as)
17	dezassete (*Br.* dezessete)	700	setecentos, (-as)
18	dezoito	800	oitocentos, (-as)
19	dezanove (*Br.* dezenove)	900	novecentos, (-as)
20	vinte	1.000	mil
21	vinte e um, uma	2.000	dois mil
22	vinte e dois, duas	1.000.000	um milhão
23	vinte e três	2.000.000	dois milhões
24	vinte e quatro	1.000.000.000	mil milhões
25	vinte e cinco	1.000.000.000	um bilhão

* With numbers above 100

A period is used instead of a comma to separate numbers of four or more digits. A comma is used to separate a whole number and a decimal.

7.532.817   7,532,817   **43,2**   43.2

One and two have both masculine and feminine forms, used whenever those numerals appear.

quarenta e duas mesas	42 tables
cento e uma casas	101 houses

Numbers in the hundreds also have two forms:

duzentas caravanas	200 trailers
oitocentas e cinqüenta e duas cervejas	852 beers

Above one thousand, numbers are always expressed in thousands and hundreds, and not as multiples of a hundred (as in the English "twelve hundred fifty"). The word *e* ("and") appears between hundreds, tens, and single digits.

cento e oitenta e dois	182

E appears after thousands in the following circumstances only:

1. When the thousand is followed by a numeral from 1–100.
2. When the thousand is followed by a numeral from 200–999, if the last two numbers are zeros.

quatro mil e sessenta e cinco	4.065
oito mil e quinhentos	8.500
mil novecentos e noventa e cinco	1.995
três mil quatrocentos e trinta	3.430

Ordinal Numbers

1st	**primeiro (-a, -os, -as)**	17th	**décimo sétimo**
2nd	**segundo**	18th	**décimo oitavo**
3rd	**terceiro**	19th	**décimo nono**
4th	**quarto**	20th	**vigésimo**
5th	**quinto**	21st	**vigésimo primeiro**
6th	**sexto**	22nd	**vigésimo segundo**
7th	**sétimo**	30th	**trigésimo**
8th	**oitavo**	40th	**quadragésimo**
9th	**nono**	50th	**qüinquagésimo**
10th	**décimo**	60th	**sexagésimo primeiro**
11th	**décimo primeiro**	70th	**septuagésimo**
12th	**décimo segundo**	80th	**octogésimo**
13th	**décimo terceiro**	90th	**nonagésimo**
14th	**décimo quarto**	100th	**centésimo**
15th	**décimo quinto**	1000th	**milésimo**
16th	**décimo sexto**		

Ordinals may be abbreviated by using the appropriate number, plus the last vowel of the number (*o* or *a*). This is clearly seen in addresses:

Moro no *12° (décimo segundo)* **andar.**   I live on the 12th floor.

Ordinals agree in number and gender with the noun to which they refer. In the compound versions (*décimo primeiro, décimo segundo, vigésimo primeiro,* etc.), both parts of the number agree.

A décim*a* **quint***a* **janel***a*.   The fifteenth window.

Ordinals are not used very frequently in Portuguese beyond ten, except in mailing addresses.

In reference to popes, royalty, and centuries, ordinals are used up to ten, and from there on, cardinal numbers are introduced. In both cases, the numbers follow the titles.

João Primeiro	John the First
o século nono	the ninth century
Manuel Doze	Manuel the Twelfth
o século vinte	the twentieth century

Fractions

1/2	**um meio**	1/6	**um sexto**
1/3	**um terço**	1/7	**um sétimo**
1/4	**um quarto**	1/8	**um oitavo**
3/4	**três quartos**	1/9	**um nono**
1/5	**um quinto**	1/10	**um décimo**

Arithmetical Signs

+	*e, mais*	**adição**	$3 + 2 = 5$	**três mais dois são cinco**
−	*menos*	**subtração**	$9 - 6 = 3$	**nove menos seis dão três**
×	*vezes*	**multiplicação**	$2 \times 2 = 4$	**dois vezes dois são quatro**
÷	*dividido por*	**divisão**	$10 \div 2 = 5$	**dez dividido por dois dá cinco**
=	*são, dá, dão,*			
	é igual a			

somar	to add	**multiplicar**	to multiply
subtrair	to subtract	**dividir**	to divide

Dimensions

Ter, ser, and *medir* are verbs used in measurements.

Nouns		Adjectives	
a altura a elevação	} height	alto	high, tall
o comprimento a extensão	} length	comprido longo	} long
a largura	width	largo	wide
a profundidade	depth	profundo	deep
a espessura a grossura	} thickness	espesso grosso	} thick

A sala tem três metros de *comprimento* **e dois de** *largura.*	The room is three meters long by two meters wide.
O mar tem duas braças de *profundidade.*	The sea is two fathoms deep.
A casa mede sete metros de *elevação.*	The house is seven meters high.

Metric Measures

o hectare	hectare
o quilograma	kilogram
o quilo	kilo
o quilómetro	kilometer
o metro	meter
o litro	liter

Other Units of Measure

a polegada	inch	o quartilho	pint
o pé	foot	um galão	gallon
a jarda	yard	a libra	pound
a milha	mile	a tonelada	ton

Geometry

Plane surfaces

a linha	line	**o rectângulo**	rectangle
o ângulo	angle	**o rombóide**	rhomboid
o ângulo reto	right angle	**o círculo**	circle
o triângulo	triangle	**o diâmetro**	diameter
o quadrado	square	**o raio**	radius

Solids

o cubo	cube	**a pirâmide**	pyramid
o cilindro	cylinder	**o cone**	cone
a esfera	sphere	**o prisma**	prism
o hemisfério	hemisphere		

32. Letters

Portuguese correspondence, particularly for business purposes, is extremely formal, and great care should be taken when composing a letter. Old-fashioned forms of address are commonplace, as are traditional opening and closing phrases. Many letters contain abbreviated forms of these often lengthy expressions.

Parts of a Letter

Headings

Nova Iorque, Estados Unidos, 7 de julho* de 19___

Rua 5 de Outubro, 32-3° esq., Lisboa

Rio, 22 de janeiro de 19___

Addresses

Senhor José Pereira
Rua Coronel Silva Telles, 36
CEP 13070-000 Campinas–SP (São Paulo)
Brasil

Sra. Dona Aliete Lopes
Av. da República, 55
Bairro de Sant'Ana
Oporto
Portugal

Telecomunicações Portugal
Sede: Pr. da Espanha, 42-3°
1831 Lisboa
Portugal

Salutations

Personal Letters:

Querido (-a) amigo (-a)	Dear Friend
Querido Miguel	Dear Michael
Cara Graça	Dear Grace

*Note that months of the year may or may not be capitalized.

Formal Letters:

Prezado senhor	Dear Sir
Estimada senhora	Dear Madam
Amigo e Senhor	Dear Sir

Business Letters:

Amigos e Srs.	Dear Sirs
Exmos. Senhores	Dear Sirs

Opening Phrases for Business Correspondence

Venho por estes meios comunicar . . .	I am writing to inform . . .
Agradeço e acuso recepção da v/ carta de . . .	I thank you and acknowledge receipt of your letter dated . . .
Em resposta a v/carta de 18 (de Dezembro, do corrente), queria informar . . .	In reply to your letter of the 18th (of December, this year), I would like to inform . . .
Sem notícias de V. Exias. há bastante tempo, venho por este meio comunicar-vos . . .	As I have not heard from you for some time, I write to inform you . . .
Levamos ao conhecimento de V. Exia. que . . .	We would like to bring to your attention that . . .
Muito gratas lhes ficaremos se nos informarem sobre . . .	We would be very grateful if you could inform us about . . .

Closing Phrases for Business Correspondence

Sem mais assunto de momento, subscrevo-me com a mais elevada consideração.	With no further business for the moment, I remain most sincerely yours.
Sempre ao dispor de V. Exia., subscrevemo-nos com especial estima . . .	Always at your disposition, we remain faithfully yours . . .
Aguardando o favor da s/resposta, somos muito atenciosamente . . .	Awaiting your reply, we remain sincerely yours . . .
Agradecendo desde já as informações que nos irão enviar, somos com consideração . . .	Thanking you for the information that you are going to forward, we remain yours faithfully . . .
Sempre às ordens, subscrevo-me . . .	Always at your service, I remain . . .
Gratos por todos os v/favores, subscrevemo-nos com sincera estima . . .	With thanks for all your help, we remain sincerely yours . . .

Endings

Personal Letters:

Com saudades de ti	Missing you
Um abraço	A big hug
Beijos, Beijinhos	Kisses

Formal/Business Letters:

Com os meus (os nossos) cumprimentos	With my (our) compliments
De V. Sas. atenciosamente	Yours truly; Sincerely
De V. Exia. atentamente	Yours truly; Sincerely

Common Abbreviations in Letters

Av.	**avenida**	avenue
Ca., Compa., Cia.	**companhia**	company
D.	**dom** (*Port.*)	title of respect (*man*)
Da.	**dona**	title of respect (*woman*)
dto.	**(lado) direito**	right (side)
esqo.	**(lado) esquerdo**	left (side)
Exmo., Exmo	**Excelentíssimo**	Excellent (Sir)
Ilmos., Il.^{mos}	**Ilustríssimos**	Excellent (Sirs)
Lda., Ltda., Lt.^{da}	**Limitada**	Limited
Lx., Ls.^{a}	**Lisboa**	Lisbon
m/	**meu(s), minha(s)**	my
n/	**nosso (-a, -os, -as)**	our
n,^{o} n.^{o}	**número**	number
p./p/	**por**	for, in behalf of
pr., P.	**praça**	square
P. S.	**Post Scriptum**	P.S.
R.	**rua**	street
s/	**seu(s), sua(s)**	his, her, your
S. A., S/A	**Sociedade Anónima**	Inc.
S. E. O.	**Salvo erro e omissão**	errors and omissions excepted
s.f.f.	**se faz favor** (*Port.*)	please
Sr.	**senhor**	sir
Sra.	**senhora**	madam
v/	**vosso (-a, -os, -as)**	your
V. Exia., V. Ex.ª	**Vossa Excelência**	your Excellency
V. Sas., V. S.as, V. S.^{as}	**Vossas Senhorias**	Sirs

Examples of Formal Letters

1.

Lagos, 25 de maio de 199_

Exmos. Senhores
Da Silva & Ca. Lda.
Av. do Brasil, 32–4° esqo.
1800 Braga

Exmos. Senhores,

Venho por estes meios pedir-vos informações sobre as v/novas publicações, sobretudo aquelas que se referem à literatura chinesa moderna.

Agradecia desde já o envio do v/catálogo corrente, junto com uma tabela de preços.

Esperando para breve o favor das v/informações, subscrevo-me,

Atenciosamente,

Maria de Nunes Costa

Lagos, May 25, 199_

Da Silva & Co. Ltd.
Brasil Ave., 32–4th left
1800 Braga

Dear Sirs,

I am writing to request information about your new publications, especially those that concern modern Chinese literature.

I thank you in advance for your current catalog, as well as a price list.

I look forward to receiving your information.

Yours truly,

Maria de Nunes Costa

2.

Braga, 12 de junho de 199_

Sra. Maria de Nunes Costa
R. Teixeira Branco, 5
8350 Lagos

Estimada senhora,

Agradecemos e acusamos recepção da v/carta datada 25 de maio, na qual pede informações acerca das n/publicações.

Junto enviamos um novo catálogo com tabela de preços. Levamos ao v/conhecimento que a partir do dia 10 de julho, podemos oferecer um desconto de 5% para encomendas com valor acima de 5 mil escudos.

Aguardando o favor da v/resposta, somos

Muito atentamente,

p/da Silva & Ca. Lda.

Braga, June 12, 199_

Mrs. Maria de Nunes Costa
5, Teixeira Branco St.
8350 Lagos

Dear Madam,

We would like to thank you for your letter of May 25, in which you request information about our publications.

We are enclosing our new catalog with a price list. We would like to bring to your attention the fact that, beginning July 10, we can offer a discount of 5% on orders of more than 5,000 escudos.

We look forward to hearing from you.

Sincerely,

(On behalf of) Da Silva & Co. Ltd.

33. Idioms

A
à direita, on the right
à esquerda, on the left
a não ser que, unless
andar a cavalo, to ride a horse
andar de bicicleta, to ride a bike
andar na escola, to go to school
andar na universidade, to go to the university
ao contrário, on the contrary
ao fim, at last
ao menos, at least
ao princípio, in the beginning

B
bater boca, to argue
boca da noite, nightfall
botar a boca no mundo, to spill the beans

C
cá entre nós, just between us
cair em si, to come to one's senses
cantada, sweet-talk
casar-se com, to marry
chorar lágrimas de sangue, to cry bitterly
com a cabeça no ar, absent-minded
cortar caminho, to take a short cut

D
dar a entender, to make understood; to suggest
dar certo, to turn out right
dar com, to meet, to come across
dar-se bem com, to get along well with
dar uma volta, to go for a walk
dar um baile em alguém, to pull someone's leg

dar um passeio, to go for a walk
de cabo a rabo, from beginning to end
deixar o barco correr, to let things take their course
de maneira nenhuma, no way
de qualquer maneira, in any case, anyway
de qualquer modo, in any case, anyway
desta maneira, in this way
deste modo, in this way

E
é isso mesmo, that's it exactly
emaranhar-se, to get mixed up
está bem, okay
estar a fim de, to be in favor of
estar com pressa, to be in a hurry
estar de férias, to be on vacation
estar de negócio, to be on business
estar na moda, to be in fashion
estar num baixo-astral, to be down
estar numa bananosa, to be in a fix
estar para + *inf.*, to be about to
estar por fazer, to be waiting to be done
estar por + *inf.*, to be in favor of

F
faltam três minutos, there are three minutes left
fazer asneira, to do something stupid
fazer cerimônia, to stand on ceremony
fazer compras, to go shopping
fazer falta, to lack, to need
fazer o possível, to do one's best
ficar bem, to suit
ficar em pé, to remain standing
ficar noivo (-a), to get engaged

ficar uma bala, to get furious
foi sem querer, it was an accident

H

haja o que houver, come what may
haver de, to have to
hoje em dia, nowadays
homem de peso, influential man

I

idas e vindas, comings and goings
Imagine só! Just imagine!
implicar com alguém, to quarrel with someone
imprensa marrom, tabloid press
(ir) Como vai? How's it going?
ir andando, to get going
ir embora, to leave
ir para casa, to go home
ir ter com, to go and meet

L

lançar mão de algo, to make use of something
lá pelas tantas, in the wee hours
largar a mão em alguém, to beat someone up
lata velha, jalopy
leitura dinâmica, speed reading
ler nas entrelinhas, to read between the lines
levar a cabo, to carry out
licenciar-se, to graduate

M

Macacos me mordam! I'll be darned!
madrugador, early bird
mãe de família, wife and mother
mais a tempo, sooner
mamar numa empresa, to skim profits
mancar-se, to get the message
Manjou? Get it?
mar de rosas, bed of roses
meter a mão em, to steal

meter a unha em, to get one's hands on

N

na calada da noite, in the dead of night
nada feito, nothing doing
na hora, in the nick of time
nascer de novo, to have a close call
nego (-a), dear, darling
ninho de rato, hornet's nest, mess
Nossa! My goodness!
nunca mais, never again

P

padrão de vida, standard of living
pelo menos, at least
pensar em, to think about
pôr a mesa, to set the table
por causa de, because of
por conseqüencia, as a consequence
por fim, at last
por isso, therefore
por meios de, by means of
provar, to try; to taste

Q

Qual é? What are you up to?
Que história é essa? What's going on?
(O) que houve? What's happened?
(O) que tem? What's up?
Quem diria! Who would have thought!
quer dizer, in other words
querer dizer, to mean

R

ralhar com alguém, to tell somebody off
ranger os dentes, to grind one's teeth
rato de biblioteca, bookworm
recursos próprios, one's own resources
remar contra a maré, to go against the tide

república de estudantes, student residence

resistir ao tempo, to stand the test of time

revirar os olhos, to roll one's eyes

romper em soluços, to sob

rua sem saída, dead-end street

S

saber de cor, to know by heart

sair bem, to turn out well

sair mal, to turn out badly

se calhar, perhaps, maybe

seja como for, be that as it may

sentir-se bem, to feel well

sentir-se mal, to feel ill

ser bode expiatório, to be a scapegoat

será que, I wonder if

servir-se, to help oneself

sonhar com, to dream about

só para inglês ver, just for show

T

Tem cada um! It takes all kinds!

ter a bondade de, to be so kind as to

ter ___ anos, to be ___ years old

ter as horas, to have the time

ter azar, to be unlucky

ter bossa de, to have an aptitude for

ter cuidado, to be careful

ter culpa, to be to blame

ter fome, to be hungry

ter medo, to be afraid

ter razão, to be right

ter sede, to be thirsty

ter sono, to be sleepy

ter sorte, to be lucky

tirar alguém da lama, to pull someone up out of the gutter

V

vai-não-vai, wishy-washiness

vaivém, back and forth

vale tudo, anything goes

Vamos. Let's go.

Vamos embora. Let's leave.

veículo de propaganda, advertising medium

vende-se, for sale

Viu? Okay?

voltar a + *inf.,* to do again

voltar à vaca fria, to get back to the subject

34. Vocabulary Lists

Common Expressions

Bom dia.	Good morning.
Boa tarde.	Good afternoon.
Boa noite.	Good evening, night.
Como está?	How are you?
Tudo bem?	How's it going?
Bem, obrigado (-a)	Fine, thanks.
E você?	And you?
E o senhor?	And you?
Olá.	Hi.
Ôi. *(Br.)*	Hi.
Adeus.	Goodbye., Farewell.
Até logo.	See you later.
Até amanhã.	See you tomorrow.
Até já.	See you soon.
o senhor	Sir, Mr.
a senhora	Madam, Mrs.
faz favor	please
faça o favor de + *inf.*	please
com certeza	of course, certainly
claro	certainly
Muito obrigado (-a)	Thanks very much.
De nada.	You're welcome.
Não tem de quê.	You're welcome.
Desculpe.	Excuse me.
lamento	I'm sorry
sinto muito	I'm sorry
Com licença.	Will you excuse me?

Countries

os Estados Unidos	the United States
a Inglaterra	England
a Grã-Bretanha	Great Britain
o Brasil	Brazil
Portugal	Portugal
a França	France
a Espanha	Spain
a Alemanha	Germany
a Suiça	Switzerland
a Dinamarca	Denmark
o Japão	Japan
a China	China
a Itália	Italy
a Grécia	Greece
a África do Sul	South Africa
a Nova Zelândia	New Zealand

Languages and Nationalities

o inglês	English
o português	Portuguese
o francês	French
o espanhol	Spanish
o alemão	German
o dinamarquês	Danish
o japonês	Japanese
o chinês	Chinese
o italiano	Italian
o grego	Greek
o russo	Russian
o latim	Latin

Meals

a comida	food
a refeição	meal
o lanche	snack
o pequeno-almoço	breakfast
o café da manhã *(Br.)*	breakfast
o almoço	lunch
o jantar	dinner
a ceia	supper

Menu

a lista	menu
a ementa	menu
o cardápio *(Br.)*	menu
as entradas	appetizers
os peixes	fish dishes
as carnes	meat dishes
as sopas	soups
as saladas	salads
as sobremesas	desserts
as frutas	fruit
o vinho da casa	house wine
o pão e manteiga	bread and butter
o prato do dia	today's special
a especialidade da casa	specialty of the house
a conta	check
a gorjeta	tip
o empregado de mesa	waiter
o garçom *(Br.)*	waiter
a garçonete	waitress
assado	grilled/roasted
cozido	boiled
ao forno	baked
grelhado	grilled
frito	fried

The Table

a mesa	table
pôr a mesa	to set the table
a toalha de mesa	tablecloth
o guardanapo	napkin
o garfo	fork
a faca	knife
a colher	spoon
o prato	plate
o copo	glass
a chávena	cup
a xícara *(Br.)*	cup
o pires	saucer
o sal	salt
o saleiro	salt shaker

a pimenta	pepper
a pimenteira	pepper shaker
o açúcar	sugar
o açucareiro	sugar bowl
o vinagre	vinegar
a galheta	cruet
a cafeteira	coffeepot
a chaleira	teapot
a bandeja	tray
o descanso de copo	coaster

Food

a comida	food
algo para comer	something to eat
o pão	bread
o pãozinho	roll
a manteiga	butter
a carne	meat
o peixe	fish
os vegetais	vegetables
os legumes	vegetables
a fruta	fruit
o queijo	cheese
o biscoito, a bolacha	cookie
umas balas	hard candies
uma sandes	sandwich
um sanduíche *(Br.)*	sandwich

Meats

a carne	meat
a carne de vaca	beef
a carne de porco	pork
a vitela	veal
o carneiro	lamb
o cabrito	goat
a costeleta	chop
o coelho	rabbit
a salsicha	sausage
o chouriço	spicy sausage
o javali	wild boar

o fiambre	boiled ham
o presunto	smoked ham
o bacon,	bacon
o toucinho	
o fígado	liver
o rim	kidney
as tripas	tripe

Fowl

as aves	fowl
o pato	duck
o ganso	goose
a galinha	hen
o frango	chicken
o peru	turkey
a perdiz	partridge
a codorniz	quail

Fish

o peixe	fish
a sardinha	sardine
o bacalhau	codfish (dried)
o camarão	shrimp
as gambas	prawns
os lagostins *(Br.)*	prawns
o peixe espada	swordfish
o espadarte	sawfish
o tamboril	monkfish
os mexilhões	mussels
a lagosta	lobster
a sarda	mackerel
o linguado	sole

Vegetables

os vegetais	vegetables
os legumes	vegetables
a batata	potato
a cenoura	carrot
a cebola	onion
a couve-flor	cauliflower
a berinjela	eggplant
o alho	garlic

o pimentão	bell pepper
o alface	lettuce
o tomate	tomato
o repolho	cabbage
o repolhinho de bruxelas	Brussels sprouts
a couve-de-bruxelas	Brussels sprouts
o pepino	cucumber
as favas	beans
o feijão	beans
as ervilhas	peas
o nabo	turnip
a beterraba	beet
a salsa	parsley
a abóbora	pumpkin
os brócolos	broccoli
o milho	corn
a batata doce	sweet potato
a mandioca	cassava, yuca

Fruit

as frutas	fruit
a laranja	orange
o limão	lemon
a lima	lime
a toronja	grapefruit
a maçã	apple
a banana	banana
o damasco	apricot
o figo	fig
o morango	strawberry
a amora	blackberry
a cereja	cherry
o melão	melon
a melancia	watermelon
o pêssego	peach
a pera	pear
o ananás	pineapple
o abacaxí *(Br.)*	pineapple

Beverages

a bebida	drink
o drinque *(Br.)*	alcoholic drink
a água	water
a água mineral	mineral water
o leite	milk
o café	coffee
a bica *(Port.)*	cup of espresso
o cafezinho *(Br.)*	cup of espresso
o café com leite	café au lait
o galão *(Port.)*	milky coffee in a glass
o chá	tea
o chá com limão	tea with lemon
o chá de ervas	herbal tea
o chocolate quente	hot chocolate
a limonada	lemonade
a laranjada	orangeade
o sumo de laranja	orange juice
o suco de laranja *(Br.)*	orange juice
o vinho	wine
a cerveja	beer
com gás	carbonated
sem gás	uncarbonated
fresco	chilled
natural	at room temperature
o gelo	ice
o canudo	straw

The Human Body

o corpo	body
a cabeça	head
o cabelo	hair
o rosto	face
a testa	forehead
a sobrancelha	eyebrow
a pestana	eyelash
o olho	eye
a orelha	ear
o nariz	nose
a bochecha	cheek
a pele	skin

a boca	mouth
o lábio	lip
a língua	tongue
o dente	tooth
a barba	beard
o pescoço	neck
a garganta	throat
o ombro	shoulder
o braço	arm
o cotovelo	elbow
o pulso	wrist
a mão	hand
o dedo	finger
a unha	nail
as espadas	back
as costas	back
o peito	chest
o pulmão	lung
o coração	heart
o estômago	stomach
o fígado	liver
o rim	kidney
o quadril	hip
a perna	leg
o joelho	knee
o tornozelo	ankle
o pé	foot
o dedo do pé	toe
o osso	bone
o calcanhar	heel

The Family and Relatives

a família	family
o marido	husband
a esposa	wife
a mulher	wife
os pais	parents
o pai	father
a mãe	mother
os filhos	children
o filho	son
a filha	daughter
o irmão	brother
a irmã	sister

os avós	grandparents
o avô	grandfather
a avó	grandmother
o neto	grandson
a neta	granddaughter
os bisavós	great-grandparents
os bisnetos	great-grandchildren
os parentes	relatives
o tio	uncle
a tia	aunt
o sobrinho	nephew
a sobrinha	niece
o primo (-a)	cousin
o sogro	father-in-law
a sogra	mother-in-law
o cunhado	brother-in-law
a cunhada	sister-in-law
o genro	son-in-law
a nora	daughter-in-law
o padrasto	stepfather
a madrasta	stepmother
o enteado	stepson
a enteada	stepdaughter
o padrinho	godfather
a madrinha	godmother

The House

a casa	house
a entrada	entrance
a porta de entrada	front door
a porta traseira	back door
a sala de estar	living room
o gabinete	study
a sala de jantar	dining room
a cozinha	kitchen
o quarto	bedroom
a casa de banho	bathroom
o banheiro (Br.)	bathroom
a lareira	fireplace
a escada	stairs
a parede	wall
o chão	floor
o tecto, o teto (Br.)	ceiling
o vestíbulo	hall

o corredor	hallway
a janela	window
o quintal	backyard
o muro	outside wall
a sebe	hedge
o portão	gate
o jardim	garden
a garagem	garage
o sótão	attic
a cave	basement
o porão (Br.)	basement

Furniture

os móveis	furniture
a mesa	table
a cadeira	chair
o sofá	sofa
a poltrona	armchair
a escrivaninha	desk
a estante	bookcase
o tapete	carpet
a cortina	curtain
a lâmpada	lamp
o quadro	picture
o guarda-roupa	wardrobe
a cama	bed
o toucador	dresser
as gavetas	drawers
o fogão	stove
a geladeira	refrigerator
o espelho	mirror

Trees

a faia	beech
o freixo	ash
o olmo	elm
a oliveira	olive tree
a laranjeira	orange tree
a macieira	apple tree
a figueira	fig tree
a cerejeira	cherry tree
a amendoeira	almond tree
a mangueira	mango tree

Insects

o inseto	insect
a aranha	spider
a mosca	fly
a joaninha	ladybug
o besouro	beetle
a libélula	dragonfly
a abelha	bee
a vespa	wasp
a borboleta	butterfly
a formiga	ant
a pulga	flea
o pulgão	aphid
a barata	cockroach

Animals

o animal	animal
o bicho	animal
o cão	dog
o gato	cat
o coelho	rabbit
o rato	mouse
o camundongo *(Br.)*	mouse
a ratazana	rat
o rato *(Br.)*	rat
o elefante	elephant
o leão	lion
o tigre	tiger
a girafa	giraffe
o rinoceronte	rhinoceros

Titles

o título	title
a dama	lady
o reverendo	reverend
o duque	duke
a duquesa	duchess
o príncipe	prince
a princesa	princess
o rei	king
a rainha	queen

o imperador	emperor
a imperatriz	empress
o conde	count
a condessa	countess

The City

a cidade	city
a rua	street
a calçada	sidewalk
a avenida	avenue
a praça	square
o parque	park
o cruzamento	intersection
o semáforo	stop lights
a rotunda	traffic circle
o quarteirão	block
a estação	railway station
a doca	dock
o aeroporto	airport
o autódromo	(auto) racetrack
o hipódromo	(horse) racetrack
o estádio	stadium

The Hotel

o hotel	hotel
a recepção	front desk
o/a recepcionista	desk clerk
o gerente	manager
o groom	bellboy
o mensageiro *(Br.)*	bellboy
o carregador	porter
o porteiro	doorman
a empregada	maid
a caixa	cashier's desk
o livro de registo, registro	register
o quarto	room
com casa de banho	with private bath
com banheiro *(Br.)*	with private bath
simples	single
duplo	double
de casal	double
o chuveiro	shower

o elevador	elevator
o ascensor	elevator
a chave	key
a conta	bill

Transportation

o transporte	transportation
o carro	car
o automóvel	automobile
o autocarro	bus
o ônibus *(Br.)*	bus
o comboio	train
o trem *(Br.)*	train
o elétrico	trolley car
o bonde *(Br.)*	trolley car
o barco	boat
o avião	plane
o táxi	taxi
a bicicleta	bicycle
a motocicleta	motorcycle
a camião	truck
o caminhão *(Br.)*	truck
a balsa	ferry
a camioneta	long-distance bus

Travel

as viagens	trips
a visita	visit
a estação	station
a bilheteira	ticket office
a bilheteria *(Br.)*	ticket office
o bilhete	ticket
simples	one-way
de ida	one-way
de ida e volta	round-trip
uma reserva	reservation
a bagagem	luggage
o baú	trunk
a mala	suitcase
o lugar	seat
o passaporte	passport
o depósito de bagagem	baggage check

o cobrador	conductor
o motorista	driver
a alfândega	customs
o horário	timetable
a carruagem-cama	sleeper car
o carro-leito *(Br.)*	sleeper car
a carruagem	carriage
o cais	platform
a plataforma *(Br.)*	platform

The Car

o carro	car
o automóvel	automobile
a estação de serviço	service station
o posto de gasolina	gas station
a oficina mecânica	garage
o depósito	tank
a gasolina	gasoline
o óleo	oil
o gasóleo	diesel
o óleo diesel *(Br.)*	diesel
o ar	air
a graxa	grease
o pneu	tire
a roda	wheel
a roda volante	steering wheel
o volante *(Br.)*	steering wheel
o freio	brake
o estacionamento	parking

Geography

a geografia	geography
o continente	continent
o país	country
a ilha	island
a península	peninsula
o cabo	cape
o golfo	gulf
a baía	bay
o oceano	ocean

a costa	coast
a praia	beach
o mar	sea
o rio	river
o lago	lake
a montanha	mountain
o vale	valley
a planície	plain
o deserto	desert
a selva	jungle
o mato	jungle
a floresta	forest
o istmo	isthmus

Good Wishes

Parabéns!	Congratulations!
Feliz aniversário.	Happy birthday.
Boa viagem.	Have a good trip.
Boas férias.	Have a good vacation.
Boa sorte.	Good luck.
Deus o abençõe.	God bless you.

Tudo de bom.	All the best.
Divirta-se.	Enjoy yourself.
Feliz Natal.	Merry Christmas.
Feliz Ano Novo.	Happy New Year.
Boas Páscoas.	Happy Easter.
Boa Páscoa. *(Br.)*	Happy Easter.

Holidays

o Natal	Christmas
a véspera do Natal	Christmas Eve
o dia do Natal	Christmas Day
a véspera de Ano Novo	New Year's Eve
o dia de Ano Novo	New Year's Day
a Quarta-Feira de Cinzas	Ash Wednesday
a Semana Santa	Holy Week
a Sexta-Feira Santa	Good Friday
o Domingo de Páscoa	Easter Sunday

Index